the handsomest man in cuba

"Hop onto Ms. Chiang's handlebars and enjoy a magical adventure in Castro's Cuba, a journey that can only take place on two wheels and with an open heart. With the warm tropical breeze to our backs, we pedal into the lives of a medley of fascinating, sometimes handsome, always amusing characters—and none more so than Lynette herself."
—Randy Komisar, author of *The Monk and the Riddle*

"The only time you'll put it down is when you finish it."
—Peter Sutherland, *Australian Cyclist* magazine

"Lynette Chiang has traveled more miles than a space shuttle, and here she finds herself in Cuba walking with the aplomb of a local citizen rather than an inquisitive fly on the wall. This is an excellent, inspiring tale that gives the reader a rare insight into a country about which little is known—and put over in a humorous style that leaves you wanting more."
—Phil Liggett, TV sports commentator with CBS/NBC/
Versus (USA) and Voice of the Tour de France

"This is one of the best 'on the road' travel books of this generation."
—Martin Stevenson, *The Launceston Examiner,* Australia

"If you're expecting the 'standard' bicycle travel book, you're in for a surprise. . . . But if you're looking for the bicycling equivalent of Steinbeck's *Travels with Charley,* you've found it."
—Larry Varney, co-editor, 'Bent Rider Online

the
handsomest
man in cuba

an escapade

Lynette Chiang

The Globe Pequot Press

GUILFORD, CONNECTICUT

This book was previously published in Australia and New Zealand in 2003 by Bantam.

is a registered trademark of Bike Friday, used with permission of Bike Friday/Green Gear Cycling Inc.
Lyrics to "Song for Jungle Boy" and "Excess Baggage" © 2007 by Lynette Chiang.

Text design by Lisa Reneson

Library of Congress Cataloging-in-Publication Data
Chiang, Lynette.
  The handsomest man in Cuba : an escapade / Lynette Chiang. — 1st Globe Pequot ed.
      p. cm.
  ISBN-13: 978-0-7627-4390-2
  ISBN-10: 0-7627-4390-5
  1. Cuba—Description and travel. 2. Chiang, Lynette—Travel—Cuba. 3. Bicycle touring—Cuba. I. Title.
  F1765.3.C45 2007
  972.91—dc22

                                                    2007000985

Manufactured in the United States of America
First Globe Pequot Edition/First Printing

To Lolita, the most beautiful woman in Cuba.

Contents

Foreword by Joe Kurmaskie, the Metal Cowboy ix

Muchas Gracias xi

Trip Map xii

1 A Cuban Christmas 1

2 Dry Spin 18

3 Heading West 25

4 Millennium Bugs 42

5 Land of the *Mogote* 52

6 The World's Worst Sailor 71

7 Cuba for Beginners 84

8 La Casa de Lolita 92

9 The Santiago Hustle 102

10 The Sierra Maestra Coast 117

11 The Handsomest Man in Cuba 131

12 Caught 141

13 The 55-Cent Hotel 150

14 A Seemingly Sacred Place 158

15 Guantanamera 165

16 The Last Resort 181

17 The Richest House in Cuba 196

18 Long Enough in Trinidad 206

19 A Loiter Too Far 217

20 Return to Havana 227

21 One Last Scoop 241

22 Home? 246

Bicycling in Cuba: Semi-Technical Stuff 249

About the Author 258

FOREWORD

There are very few things in this world that leave me speech-less. I'm what you might call chatty, verbally imbued, a black belt in the art of babble. Hey, it's a living. A chuckle or two to light the literary darkness; just don't ask me to make change for a twenty.

But when faced with that mug on Lynette Chiang's book cover, I shut my mouth, pausing midbite over my morning cere-al to pay homage. Here stood a gent clearly able to embrace the sublime and absurd in this world with, shall we say, a certain amount of flair.

Here stood an original. Hard as it is to avoid doing some-times, we're told repeatedly not to judge books by their covers, lest the plot police whisk us away to padded rooms brimming with thousand-page tomes containing no pictures, translated from German, with all of the covers torn off.

I've never been snatched up by these "death to pop culture" squads, but I'm told it's not pretty. Even so, I decided to pass judgment, live dangerously, and crack open Lynette's cycling escapades around Cuba. I've been burned so many times by awful journals passing themselves off as books. Still, who could ignore the come-on of that quirky gent?

Here's the thing: This book turns out to be the first two-wheeled travel adventure I've read in far too long that is more than just a pretty face. Lynette writes herself into a more colorful character than the poster boy out front and the rainbow of folks found inside each chapter. No easy feat considering that Lynette's Cuba is well stocked with lively individuals full of hopes, schemes, and a seemingly endless supply of goodwill and hospitality.

By turns introspective, charming, and thoughtful, *The Handsomest Man in Cuba* packs in what so many travel adventures discard: the emotional landscape of a country and the interior map of the person exploring it. Upon finishing this book you may want to secure the next circuitous flight to what was once called the "playground of the tropics" or avoid that island empire like head lice, but the one thing you'll feel compelled to do is follow Lynette's next adventure wherever she decides to travel.

Joe Kurmaskie
www.metalcowboy.com

Joe is the award-winning author of several best-selling story collections, including Metal Cowboy *and* Riding Outside the Lines. *In addition to his one-man show, "Metal Cowboy Mayhem," and his syndicated columns, Joe contributes to* Men's Journal, Backpacker, The L.A. Times, Bicycling, *and* The Oregonian.

MUCHAS GRACIAS

To Barney Collier, who chanced upon my first published story about Lolita in the *Tico Times,* flew to Costa Rica, and trudged up a mossy mountain to loan me his lucky Toshiba laptop, insisting that I "finish the tale." To Glenn "Murry" Richmond, who gave me a sanctuary from the madness of the city and told me to stop fooling around with things I am not good at. To Jorge Oller, who gave me a life and purpose in Costa Rica, daring to trust a wandering Aussie with the creativity of his agency, Consumer Excepcional Nazca Saatchi & Saatchi—not to mention putting up with La China JP's inexplicable need to go bikeabout . . . To Joshua Daniel and David Arnold, for expertly retouching the "Cuban Photographer." To Bike Friday, for making a bicycle that enabled me to be out of The System for so long, for so many miles, despite an incurably poor sense of direction. To Jim Hendrickson, for correcting my bad Spanish. To Jungle Boy, for inspiring my first original song. To Dennis Stuhaug, Bike Friday owner and author of Basic Essentials® *Sit-on-Top Kayaking* (Globe Pequot), who got my book to acquisitions editor Sarah Mazer Zink, who opened it up. To Steve Martin—I never thought I'd pen a word worth pondering until I heard him say "A writer says things well; a genius, well, says them."

¡Muchísimas gracias!

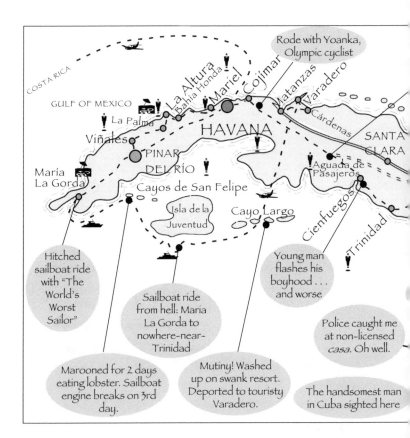

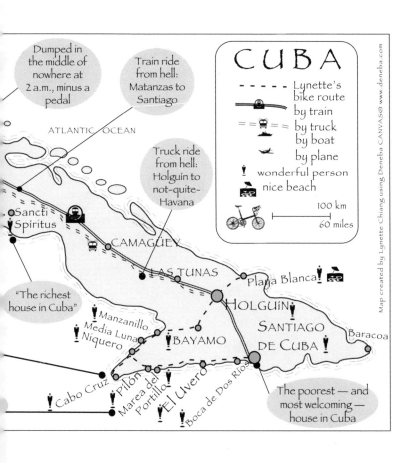

Dumped in the middle of nowhere at 2 a.m., minus a pedal

Train ride from hell: Matanzas to Santiago

ATLANTIC OCEAN

Truck ride from hell: Holguin to not-quite-Havana

CUBA

– – – – – Lynette's bike route

by train

= = = by truck

by boat

by plane

wonderful person

nice beach

100 km

60 miles

Map created by Lynette Chiang using Deneba CANVAS© www.deneba.com

Sancti Spíritus

CAMAGUEY

LAS TUNAS

Playa Blanca

HOLGUIN

SANTIAGO DE CUBA

Baracoa

"The richest house in Cuba"

Manzanillo

Media Luna

Níquero

BAYAMO

Cabo Cruz

Pilón

Marea del Portillo

El Uvero

Boca de Dos Ríos

The poorest — and most welcoming — house in Cuba

1

A CUBAN CHRISTMAS

I've landed in a small kitchen, somewhere in Havana, Cuba. I should have brought food.

The kind *señora* has offered me dinner: a toasted bread roll, fried egg on top, glass of orange soft drink. I swallow the snack whole on its way from fry pan to table. My stomach clamors for more. There is no more.

I'd read all about the scarcity of food in Cuba, where people are depicted as having barely enough to feed the family, let alone dollar-waving tourists. But in my eternal quest to travel light, I have allowed a very important item, especially for a bicycle tourist, to slip to the bottom of the list. The only thing I've stashed is a jar of pumpkin jam lovingly cooked up by my Dutch beau in Costa Rica, whose love for me would sadly sour, just like the jam, in my three-month absence.

I had met him a year earlier on the island of Bocas del Toro in Panama. We were both standing at the reception desk of the hotel where he stayed every three months when he had to leave Costa Rica to renew his visa, he being one of the perpetual tourists building a First World life in a Second World paradise.

I'd just reserved the last room. Since it had two beds, I did a quick visual reconnaissance of his tall, blonde, not-quite-thirtyness and decided it would be harmless enough to offer him the other bed and, more importantly, to halve my hotel bill.

I had always avoided blonde men. The small cross section I'd meddled with seemed possessed of a curious arrogance that I put down to the world treating them like the rare recessive gene they spring from. But I have learned to leave judgment to the judicial system and to removalists squeezing a grand piano up a stairway. It was my third year of traveling with a bicycle, a tent, and a poor sense of direction, and all along strangers of whatever color sideburns have helped me, befriended me, rescued me.

My Dutch room buddy and I quickly bonded in the way veteran transients do, very much in the moment and always mindful of the move-by date stamped in our passports. At twenty-three he had inherited money and taken the brave step of creating a life in the Caribbean jungle far from his family in the chilly, orderly European Union.

I, on the other hand, had traded life in the Australian 'burbs —complete with house, garden, fastish car, and snug relationship—for a folding bicycle, a tent, and a one-way ticket to nowhere in particular. I was thirty-four. The thirties are a difficult age, according to Gail Sheehy's *Passages* and every other self-help book I could lay my hands on to explain my inexplicable discontent with my very fortunate life. It had been a real struggle to decide to ditch my salaried working life, but an ugly stress rash that left me quarantined like a leper forced me to make some stern decisions. I had $5,000 in the bank and I figured I could last a few months and then . . . I tried not to think about the *then*.

The idea of setting out on a bicycle came to me when someone showed me a map of Great Britain with a little dotted line going from the bottom to the top. Land's End to John O'Groats, one of the classic bicycle journeys. Until I saw that map, I had never traveled alone. I was fearful of roaming outside my own postcode. I had only ridden a bicycle with a group of people on a day ride. My sense of direction was appalling. But the map was about 2 inches tall. I thought, "I can do that."

Soon after someone told me about a curious small-wheeled folding bicycle that looked like a cross between a child's BMX, an old lady's shopping bike, and something distinctly high-tech. It was called a Bike Friday, so named "in honor of Robinson Crusoe's trusty sidekick . . . unobtrusive, yet always ready and waiting," said the advertising blurb. It promised that the bike would be custom built to fit my 5-foot-nothing frame perfectly and, for all its compactness, would feel similar to a regular "big wheel" bike.

The bike was available only by mail order from some obscure little town in Oregon called Eugene. The company sent me a persuasive video and a guarantee that tried its best to convince me to order a bike without actually sitting on one. The video showed how it packed into a Samsonite-like suitcase; the makers had cleverly designed a small chassis and wheels so that the suitcase itself could be towed behind the bike like a little caboose. The footage showed rider, suitcase, and backpack arriving at the airport, the check-in clerk blissfully ignorant of the wonder concealed within. On arrival, the bike came out of the suitcase, the backpack went in, the trailer wheels were attached, and *voila*—rider, steed, and stuff pedaled off to some guidebook destination together. The best feature, claimed the video, was that the bike would fold in thirty seconds. I thought of my as-yet-underdeveloped calf muscles and knew that this feature would make it easy to accept a ride, if necessary, on cars, buses, trains, or boats.

The poor Aussie dollar made the bike an outrageous extravagance, but they would prove to be Aussie dollars well spent. The bike would be my Cadillac, Porsche, and U-Haul all rolled up into one, without the noxious fumes. I would be the engine.

• • • •

A proud and feisty Cuban woman, my hostess Maruca is clearly one of the lucky ones. The triangular blue sticker on her door identifies her apartment as a bona fide *casa particular,* or licensed guest house. Without a license, a house that accepts paying guests risks being raided and the owner slapped with a fine of ten times the $100 monthly license fee. Put another way, that's 100 times the monthly wage of most ordinary Cubans.

Maruca sits beside me and produces a large appointment book in which to record my name, passport number, and country of origin. She shuffles a large folder of papers and forms, all designed to keep the people honest, socialist, and just a little bit scared.

Although the western media seems to treat *Cuba* and *Communism* like synonyms rather than mere alliterations, state-sanctioned businesses like *casas particulares, paladares* (restaurants), 5-peso pizza stands, and cigarette-lighter refueling stations allow average Cubans to dip their toes into the balmy waters of *capitalismo.* This despite the constant reminders on radio, television, and billboards that *comunismo* is alive and well, even if Fidel Castro is less so.

In the corner a radio blasts out salsa music interspersed with patriotic messages. Cubans, like other Latino cultures, do not relish silence. In Nicaragua I was told that silence makes one think of "the troubles." Too many times I have stopped to gaze upon a silent, sweeping vista, only to have the mood shattered by a backing track of crackly Latino rap.

The narrow concrete balcony of Maruca's *casa* overlooks Vedado, one of the wealthier districts in Havana. Seven floors below, the main road runs down to Havana's crumbling *malecón*, or oceanfront boulevard. Old rusting American cars putter along this stretch intermittently, carrying locals across town for 50 cents. The cabbies, too, risk being fined two arms and two legs if the pasty mug of a *turista* is spotted by the police through their car windows. For tourists there are shiny, air-conditioned orange taxis with shampooed carpets and Kleenex and English-speaking drivers in uniform, who charge ten times the local fare for the same journey.

I landed at Maruca's by accident. On the flight from Costa Rica I had met Alfredo, an El Salvadoran on his third visit to Cuba. He has always stayed with Maruca, and her family house has become his home away from home. I remembered the El Salvadorans as the warmest and most sincere people I had met, so I felt very optimistic about tagging along behind him.

Alfredo waited patiently and courteously at customs while the officials went through every single item of my luggage, slowly turning things over in their hands as if examining ancient artifacts. My torch, bicycle pump, and never-go-moldy travel towel sent them oohing and ahhing. There were cocked eyebrows and subtle suggestions about slipping them a little something to let me through the gate. They didn't even bat an eyelid at Alfredo's giant third suitcase, which revealed a freshly stocked supermarket aisle of goodies when he finally opened it.

"How much money are you carrying?" asked one of the officials.

I hesitated.

"Dos mil," I mumbled out of the corner of my mouth, hoping he didn't hear "two thousand dollars." One month's salary for me, six years' salary for a Cuban doctor. An obscene amount of cash for a cyclist to bring to this country strapped to her thigh.

Yet I would be gone from my privileged foreigner post as creative director of a Costa Rican advertising agency for three months, and a quote from some corporation was ringing in my ears: "If we can do without you for three months, we can do without you."

I hoard this stash like it is the last pay-packet I will ever have.

• • • •

Maruca's apartment has three rooms that normally rent for $25 a night each, but after pleading poor, as I do instinctively when cycle touring, regardless of my financial circumstances, she lowers the rate to $15. I have actually budgeted for less than $10 a night.

One dingy floor up I meet Tito, a bespectacled, birdlike Spaniard who is also preparing to circumnavigate the island by bicycle. He purchased locally a very decent touring bike for $90 and plans to tour for several months. Tito is another vagrant who escaped Europe and is now searching for whatever people search for when they sell their furniture and buy a one-way ticket to the boonies.

We head out together to get a Cuban pizza, a 6-peso disk of rubbery cheese and red coloring sold from a hole in a condemned building. I see *capitalismo* glinting through the hole. With a Cuban peso worth about 5 cents, that makes the 30-cent snack the deal of the decade for tourists. The exact same pizza at a tourist restaurant, air-conditioned and fluorescent-lit, costs twenty times more.

• • • •

The next day Tito, Alfredo, and I hail a local taxi and head off to the central park in front of the Capitolio, a huge dome-topped edifice modeled on the Capitol in Washington, D.C.

In the sweeping, half-empty plaza, a man is taking photos with a contraption built from found objects. He's worthy of a photo himself: an old, stringy codger with faded ball cap, matching red sneakers, and lips permanently contorted into an *O* shape by the stub of a fat cigar.

To take a picture, he covers the lens with a detergent-bottle lid, removes it for a few seconds, and then replaces it. The developing process involves clipping the negative to a board with the word CUBA written on it in reverse. He then dips the whole thing into a rusty tin of black liquid. Minutes later the tiny Kodak moment appears, looking like a page from your great-great-great-grandmother's brag book.

He must be doing well—he has a nice belt buckle. He sells us three copies of the shot for a dollar. It seems to fade even as I admire it.

We decide to change some dollars for pesos and wait patiently in line at an official exchange house. Suddenly, we notice a dude in a dazzling white suit and Panama hat motion to us from the corner. His attire is so obvious that I figure he must be street legal. He fans his wads of dollar and peso bills like a card sharp and gives us the Latino "lip point," which I recognize from my time in Costa Rica: a simultaneous puckering of the lips and thrusting of the chin in our general direction that translates to "Whassup?" Thrusting the chin in another direction means "over there."

His ploy works, and we drift on over to his turf.

"How much?" he asks.

I do a quick calculation, recalling some advice I read somewhere to change no more than $5 to $10 to pesos at a time, because a little peso goes a long way.

"Twenty dollars," I reply, feeling extravagant.

He begins counting, and so do I. At 20 Cuban pesos to the dollar, there is a lot of counting to do. When he gets to 380, he stops and I am still counting. He clears his throat and starts over.

Next, I ask him to change my $50 bill into two $20 bills and 100 Cuban pesos, which he hands to me. Then I absentmindedly walk off with the loot without actually handing him my $50 bill. Of course he catches me, and I guffaw that I obviously have a talent for his job. He does not appear to appreciate this jest.

We walk all the way to the *malecón*, where the Straits of Florida are smashing up and over the seawall leading all the way back to Vedado. Anywhere in the First World, an oceanfront boulevard like this would be tarted up with glitzy bars, hotels, and cafes. Here, the boulevard is one long colonial demolition site snaking its way around the seafront, punctuated by faded signs announcing a little eatery here or a watch repair shop there, somewhere in the rubble.

As we gaze out to sea, a young black man approaches us

with a Cuban flag. In ten minutes he's invited us to share in his family's Christmas celebrations in Santiago de Cuba, the country's second-largest city. I read that it's a hellish twelve-hour train ride all the way to the far east of the island. We talk about life in Cuba, and I ask him directly if he usually invites total strangers to his house—why, I could be an axe murderer!

He grins. "I am a junior champion wrestler, and I fear nothing," he says. Then he explains, somewhat softly, that Cubans who have no access to dollars in order to buy cool threads for the millennium celebrations will instead offer *amistad* (friendship) to tourists and then maybe, just maybe . . .

I consider his unabashed invitation for a full two minutes. As we banter, the possibilities tick over in my mind. I run a mental movie of possible outcomes, based on my chaperone being this twenty-something hustler: long train ride, meeting the family, toothy smiles, dinner-table Spanglish, standing on a rock gazing out in the direction of his pointing finger, hanging out with his skateboarding buddies minus the skateboards, handing out money . . . all very pleasant. "Thanks but no thanks," I think but don't say.

"Do you think I was a bit too direct with that young guy?" I ask Alfredo as we walk on.

"Direct?" He chokes on his drink. "Very."

As we walk, Alfredo gives me a verbal essay on the standard of living here, based on what he has observed on his previous visits.

Doctors in Cuba are the elite, he says, and earn an official $25 a month. Despite appearances to the contrary, many Cubans do have access to dollars from second jobs, or they run illicit businesses or receive cash from relatives who live in Miami.

"Once upon a time, no Cuban was allowed to possess dollars," he said. "Now there are little exchange houses everywhere to enable them to do just that. The problem is to find the money to change in the first place. It is easy to spot the Cubans with access to dollars: Simply glance at their shoes and clothes. If neither have holes, that means they have dollars."

I do notice that despite the holiness of dollarless poverty, I see no adult or child who seems hungry or desperate. Everyone seems to belong to someone, somewhere. I note that a sense of belonging has eluded me for as long as I can remember.

• • • •

On the way back to the apartment, we stop at a noisy, flag-waving gathering. Nearly everyone wears T-shirts bearing the face of Elián González, the little boy who fled with his mother on a makeshift boat to Florida. His mother drowned, but Elián, strapped to some inner tubes, miraculously survived and was hauled from the raging seas. The boy is the center of a lengthy U.S.–Cuba custody battle. *SALVEMOS A ELIÁN* reads the slogan: We will save Elián. Huge billboards bearing his elfin face are displayed around the city, right alongside the propaganda posters like *CREEMOS EN LA REVOLUCIÓN*: We believe in the Revolution.

Because I have not read a newspaper in months, I heard about this affair only via e-mail, from an American acquaintance who told me to be "very careful" when I set foot on Cuban soil.

"If I were you, I'd tie an Australian flag to the back of your bike and practice saying 'G'day mate' in as broad an Australian accent as possible," he advised.

I've noticed this kind of paranoia before among Americans, who seem trapped in a land of litigation and prenuptial agreements, guns concealed in clutch purses and schoolbags, and grave concerns about teachers putting a comforting arm around children of the opposite sex who have fallen and hurt themselves. I meet Americans fearful of setting foot in Nicaragua, lest they be chased back to the nearest border with machetes. In Nicaragua I discovered a humble but wise people, aware that an American person and the American government are not one and the same. I can only conclude that people who have suffered develop a kind of X-ray vision and see that blood is the same color—no matter where you come from.

A pair of Cuban men approach me, and after a short chat about the demonstration, one of the men removes his Elián T-shirt and slips it over my head.

"No, no," I protest, knowing that a new T-shirt is like a new pair of hole-free jeans, but he insists that I keep it and gives me his address.

"Twenty-three days now and no word. We can only hope he comes back," says one. I sense that his feelings about Elián are sincere, like the little boy was his own brother.

This is my first glimpse of the profound love a Cuban has for his country and fellow countrymen. I'd read about it in the Web page memoirs of others who'd traveled here and ventured beyond the resorts catering to culturally indifferent tourists. It is a love that is powerful and unique yet, as I quickly discover, not invincible. The encroaching dollar is making sure of that.

• • • •

Upstairs in Tito's apartment Emparo, the landlady, invites me to join in their Christmas dinner, and I accept. It's a simple affair of roast chicken, boiled *yuca* root (a dense, potatolike vegetable), rice and beans, and salad, all prepared with a healthy scoop of pig fat, which Emparo's son and cook gleefully waves under my nose. The lard is stored in a large, screw-top jar; it is gray-white and resembles the melted wax of cheap, smoky candles. He scoops it out with a spatula and spreads it thickly on almost all the ingredients of the meal. I kinda wish I hadn't stuck my nose in the kitchen.

The seven people in the room swiftly polish off all the food in sight while glued to the blaring television set. They finish with a slice of *torrón,* a delicate sweet made from ground almonds, which Tito brought all the way from Spain. I wish I had something edible to bring to the table. But I don't.

• • • •

Around 9:30 P.M. the room suddenly empties.

People have left the table midmouthful to view the currently running soap opera known as *la novela*—the treacly *Days of Our Lives* of Latino television, churned out nightly from Mexico or Brazil. Almost every Cuban watches it as if it's the story of his personal destiny. In Emparo's sitting room the volume is turned up to an eardrum-perforating level. I step out onto the balcony and look down at the previously bustling street. It is deserted.

• • • •

La novela ends at 10:30 P.M. Suddenly there is movement in the streets and in the living room. The party resumes. Tito suggests that we go to the Jazz Café, a fancy hotel nightspot, and grab a drink.

As we walk along the street, the nutty Spaniard decides to experiment.

"Did you see *la novela* tonight?" he asks passersby who are strolling arm in arm in the moonlight.

"Of course!" comes the unanimous reply.

"So how did it end?"

"Well, the boyfriend went back to the farm, and the son resolved his differences with his mother," is the second unanimous reply. So unanimous that the experiment becomes boring very quickly, and after the tenth *vox pop* interview, I wish Tito would just drop it.

We arrive at an imposing, modern hotel jutting out from a flat, rubble-strewn expanse of nothing much. We ascend the granite stairs to the Jazz Café. We could be stepping inside any big-city nightclub with curved walls and moody lighting, but this one is packed with beautiful Cubans chatting with largely unbeautiful foreigners. Inoffensive jazzy tunes emanate from the bandstand. The drink menu looks cheap enough: $2.50 for a piña colada, the most expensive cocktail. But the drink arrives in a small glass tumbler the size of the cap of a pill bottle, a single swig. I am determined to make it last.

"*Putas,* all of them!" observes Tito.

He points to the leggy and coiffed Cuban girls in short skirts and stiletto heels that taper into luridly painted toenails. *Puta,* I am told, translates directly to "bitch" and a bit less directly to "whore."

"Even that one over there?" I ask, motioning to a prim, secretarial type in a demure beige suit and sensible shoes. She is chatting amiably to a couple of girlfriends.

"All of 'em. Time for another experiment."

With that the wicked Spaniard gets up and approaches a delectable *chica* at a nearby table that she shares with an imposing black man in a blacker suit. From our safe distance we observe that she responds to Tito in a very friendly and attentive fashion. The Man in Black gets off his stool and moves toward the bar.

"See what I mean?" remarks Professor Tito upon returning to our table.

"If a girl is with a man and she is a *puta,* she will respond in the manner in which she did, and her bodyguard or pimp will soon disappear. Otherwise, she'll just snub you."

Now, I must admit that I tend to respond in a friendly fashion to whoever happens to approach me, no matter who I am with, so I may well have been mistaken for a *puta* many times over, albeit one with a poor nose for business.

• • • •

Back at the apartment, Emparo's hubby, Sergio, is well tanked and merry on the local anesthetic. He brings out a dusty box containing the dozen or so medals of honor he obtained throughout his career as a soldier, most impressively his accolade from the war in Angola in 1988.

As I was told about it, U.S.-backed South Africa invaded Marxist-led Angola, and Cuba was summoned to help out the besieged. The story goes that Fidel had developed such a crack military force that South Africa was forced to hastily retreat, and both Angola and Namibia soon became independent. Nelson Mandela later thanked Cuba for its pivotal role in the defeat of apartheid.

For a memorable photo shoot, Tito and I persuade Sergio to take all the medals out of the box and pin them on his lovingly preserved military uniform, an activity that clearly thrills the proud former colonel. It's a big job. The medals are individually pinned to a velvet ridge, and it takes some time and effort to prize each one away. They have not been out on parade for years. But Tito hops from one foot to the other, egging the old colonel on, and our war hero is determined to have the photo include the special cross that is hidden separately under his bed, as well as his old, but very shiny, army-issue shoes.

The family bulldog is an aged mutt with one front leg amputated because of cancer. The impish Tito persuades the master and his dog to pose together, the war hero standing proudly with his battle-scarred best friend, a shot of heroic proportions.

"¡Qué bueno!" grins Tito, down on both knees as he frames the shot.

"Please, do not show those pictures to anyone," implores the old colonel, "in case it gets back here."

Why strutting one's stuff for risking life and limb for king and country would be dangerous, only a Cuban in a changing Cuba would know.

• • • •

We discover in the evening the best deal of all: a movie in the local cinema for 1 peso, or 5 cents. In fact, because the air-conditioning is not working, the woman behind the cashier window insists on charging me 20 percent less, which creates a mass of tiny subpeso coins in my pocket.

Nearby, the angular concrete silhouette of the Coppelia ice-cream parlor rises from the shrubs like a misplaced sphinx. In the ensuing weeks I will see different architectural incarnations of Cuba's premier ice creamery, each one a brutal confection resembling one of the triple-scoop specials stuck with wafers, studded with nuts, and melting. It looks like the architect was given uncharacteristically free reign, perhaps gleaning his inspiration from black-and-white footage of the Sydney Opera House, Gaudí's Sagrada Familia, and *Battlestar Galactica* seen on Cuba's only television soap opera channel, all the while deeply inhaling the illicit weed.

Inside, however, the experience is distinctly watered-down vanilla. An overstaffed counter dispenses mushy scoops of something cold and clammy in little steel cups to the smattering of patrons seated at the metal tables in wire chairs. The flavor of the day is melon. For the adventurous there are also strawberry and chocolate. Häagen-Dazs it's not, but we agree that the place has a unique flavor.

The movie we're seeing is a renowned Cuban classic called *Fresa y Chocolate* (*Strawberry and Chocolate*), a complicated tale about homosexuality, individuality, and The System. Or that's what I deduce from simply observing the various couplings, uncouplings, shouting, and pouting.

I understand practically none of the movie, partly because of the poor audio system, which sounds little better than a transistor radio in a bucket of water, but mostly because of my failure to grasp the Cuban dialect, a fast and furious version of Spanish with entire paragraphs jammed into a single breath. We are seated with a small group of Spaniards from Madrid whom Tito has befriended.

The Spaniards shake their heads. "We couldn't understand much of it either," they say, when I managed to decipher *their* accents.

Tito, the unrelenting tour guide, announces that he will take us to eat "the best fried chicken in Havana." He leads us to a government-run cafeteria, a simple fluorescent-lit room with a few canned foodstuffs for sale, along with some pasta sauce, packets of pasta, bars of guava jelly, and, strangely, bars of peanut *torrón,* or peanut brittle. The chicken itself is unremarkable and costs around $1.20 a quarter serving. There are no napkins to catch the dripping grease. Here I discover a new kind of nonalcoholic beverage called Maltina, a black sticky liquid with a creamy head made from what is left at the bottom of the barrel in the beer-production process. It resembles Guinness stout but tastes of watered-down maple syrup.

The Cuba I had read about tasted of fine cigars, smooth *mojitos,* beans and rice, and tropical sea air, with a backing beat of Ry Cooder's *Buena Vista Social Club.*

The Cuba I am tasting now is a stomach full of greasy chicken, an ersatz pizza disk, and a slice of chewy guava jelly. And yet I am eager for the next course.

2

DRY SPIN

Boxing Day, which is the day after Christmas Day in Australia, does not exist in Cuba.

Back home it is the day when people put their new battery-operated fans, marble cheese platters, tins of nasty, cheap shortbread and plaques mounted with rubber fish that sing "Take Me to the River" back into their gift boxes for exchange at the store, or for regifting at a future birthday party.

Few Cubans have the money to give a gift that would actually come in a box, and it was not until recently that December 25 became a day to lay down tools, rest, reflect, and overeat along with the outside western world. Christmas Day was not a holiday in Cuba because it interfered with the cane-cutting season.

I spend most of Boxing Day sorting through my cycle-touring equipment and restudying my maps, a futile exercise given my poor sense of direction. I know I will be screeching to a halt after the first left and having to look at the map again. I open the suitcase trailer and shake my folding bike out of its Houdini-like contortion, mount its urban assault gear (fenders, rack, lights), and take it for a spin out to Miramar, the posh embassy suburb west of almost-as-posh Vedado.

The first thing I notice is that my witty LONG LOAD sign has been torn off my suitcase. The suitcase can be towed as a trailer, and the sign was an attempt at a little passing-lane humor to encourage charitable treatment from overtaking trucks. The fact that it has been torn off is yet another reminder to remove anything that is not riveted to my luggage before going through check-in.

The second things out of whack are the gears—the Costa Rican bike shop where I had the bike serviced clearly did not know how to adjust a three-speed hub gear. Neither do I, but I eventually work out that you have to pop it into third gear before fiddling with the tautness of the cable.

Thus, the "dry spin" is a necessary pretrip meander on any bike tour of more than a few days; you get to iron out the glitches before they become hitches.

• • • •

Miramar is a desolately upscale place. Pristine, oversize embassy homes flank wide, empty streets. No snuffling stray dogs, no discarded ice-cream wrappers decorating the curb. Pedaling slowly along the ocean boulevard, I am reminded of wandering through scene after silent scene of a computer game without the right tools or insights to open any of the tightly locked doors.

I see a parking lot that terminates with a roughly built brick wall, into which a ragged hole has been smashed for someone to gaze out to the sea—the sea that sidles up to Florida, the Forbidden Land. Two men miraculously appear from the ruins and tell me that I am not allowed to enjoy the view in that spot.

I imagine they are plainclothes police planted here to deter any Cuban from even entertaining the thought of swimming across to the Other Side. I move on.

I decide that Miramar offers me nothing. By now I am hungry, the familiar pangs of the cyclist's stomach hitting me every hour on the hour since I arrived in Cuba. I ask for directions to one of the elusive *paladares,* or private restaurants. A woman offers to chaperone me to a condemned-looking building on a side street. We pick our way across a dark ground floor littered with rusting iron and concrete, ascend some wet cement steps, feel our way along a wall, and then snake through a rotting wooden corridor and up a rotting flight of stairs. By this time I half expect to find crack cocaine on the menu, but we emerge onto a rooftop terrace to the familiar, comforting appearance of a restaurant—that is, little tables and chairs and a thatch-roof bar.

El Recanto is a popular secret, and I am told there will be a one-hour wait. The food costs only a couple of dollars a plate— perfect. The menu seems to be little more than various permutations of rice, beans, and fried pork, but it smells mighty good after my breakfast of an apple and a greasy pizza disk. To encourage speedier delivery I order takeaway rice and vegetables and drink a Maltina. Then I notice the unmistakable pallor of a foreigner leaning against the bar. Marsaille is a twenty-something born-again vagrant, a Frenchman who has spent the past five years drifting from country to country, living off his construction skills. "Eet pays well," he says, sucking on his soda.

I think of my computer science degree and my time as an advertising copywriter, and how these cerebral skills seem patently useless in this place, in the real, hard world where most people eat to live and rarely vice versa.

Not for the first time I find myself wishing I was a bloke, a side of beef with a hard hat, matted pits, scary tatts, and a mug that murmurs "Don't mess with me."

I wish I could build a house, one that would not sag in a corner because I did not measure the concrete quite right or something.

I recall Eddie, an English friend who'd fled his home country, a failing business, and impending heart attack to rebuild a little stone farmhouse in a blustery corner of southwest Ireland, saying, "See that corner? It's probably not square, but . . . it only has to last my lifetime."

I also remember Peter, the resilient hostel owner/fisherman/builder living on the raging seafront not far from Eddie, telling me what it meant to feel secure: "Above the crust of the earth, it's all bullshit." He was stacking freshly dug peat moss in a huge pile for the coming winter's fire. "If you can fish the sea, dig the earth, and build with your hands, you will always feel secure."

• • • •

I rise early the next day to extend my one-month tourist visa to two months, a tedious day-waster no matter what country you're in. The procedures always seem to change, as if deliberately trying to keep writers of guidebooks in business. I stand in line at the austere *migración* office for half an hour before a German tourist kindly shows me the two postage stamps you must buy beforehand at a bank down the road. Dang.

Back in the line I meet Charlotte, a born-again vagrant of the Danish kind who'd left her stylish apartment, cozy relationship, and enviable job as editor of the lifestyle section of a

Copenhagen newspaper in order to see how the other nine-tenths live. She fell in love with her Cuban dance teacher, a man she said was more beautiful on the inside than on the outside, and for whom she was on the brink of selling up her previous life to join him and salsa into the sunset. She just had to renew her visa to find out for sure.

By late afternoon we are both gazing out to sea in the garden bar of the palatial Hotel Nacional.

We sip $4.00 watery piña coladas and talk about life and quitting jobs and changing everything on a whim. Her eyes shine when she speaks of the love she has found within the walls of a simple Havana apartment with none of the comforts of Copenhagen. A few months later I would hear that she returned to Denmark. Even later I would discover that she married her Cuban and took him back to Denmark, and that a little baby was born.

"How did you . . . decide?" I asked her on e-mail. She never replied.

After one drink I pedal off and find a bicycle parking lot, actually the front yard of someone's house, where you can have your bike guarded for 2 pesos (10 cents). Another capitalist microventure, though I wonder if a license is required. An old man with a creased face appears from behind a bush and motions with a bony hand that it is not necessary to use my Kryptonite Fort Knox Megalock. But I take no chances.

• • • •

I set out on foot for one of the largest supermarkets in town to buy whatever provisions I can for my trip. Edificio Focsa is a far cry from the Tescos and Sainsburys on which I'd thoroughly spoilt during my time in England. It resembles what I always imagined a Russian supermarket to be, having three narrow aisles of tomato salsa (three different brands ranging in price from 55 cents to $1.80), rice, pasta (different shapes), expensive canned tuna, a variety of imported second-grade biscuits, toilet paper, soap, and a separate counter selling fresh chicken. And that's all.

I buy two Tetra packs of tomato salsa, four 200-gram bags of penne pasta, a can of tuna, and a bottle of water. The supermarket sells cigarettes, a foul, throat-rasping kind made from the dregs of the tobacco-factory floors, but curiously, I cannot find matches. A veteran of at least five solo tours, I have packed everything I will ever need except the waterproof matches.

As I leave the supermarket, I hear a hissing sound. I turn around to see the boy who packed my grocery bags holding up my wallet between his fingers. It contains $100—ten times the average monthly Cuban wage. I thank him profusely and make a mental note to pay more attention. Earlier that day I had left my airline ticket wallet sitting on the counter of the office where I delayed my departure date.

In my travels I have learned that leaving one's wallet or document bag lying idly on a counter is a sure sign of being floored by new surroundings. It's a slap across the face and a warning to slow down, get oriented, get centered, and gather your wits, because you're going to need them.

When I finally get back to the apartment and haul my bike through the portcullis of Maruca's security door, a woman I've never met before is waiting for me with a six-pack of match boxes and a liter of alcohol for my camping stove. For these supplies she charges me $1.00 each.

And no, I cannot buy just one box of matches, which is all I need.

They say America is the land of service, but in Cuba you only have to half-mutter something in your sleep, and someone will appear at your door with the item—or at least they'll make a supreme effort to find it, for a crisp dollar bill.

And now, with my life-support system ready to go, it's time to leave the city comforts of Havana and see the real Cuba.

3

HEADING WEST

Maruca is alarmed. "You will be knocked down by *borrachos* [drunk Cubans]. Why don't you stay for New Year's Eve, and leave on the first?"

I load up my bike as it leans against the dresser. Though her words make sense, I am suffering from caged-ferret syndrome, the result of being cooped up in a small apartment with bars on every window. Once I pull on my red and black Lycra cycling gear, it sets my internal wheels in motion.

I used to detest cycling clothes. They seemed to be designed by the same people who make clown apparel, minus the neck frills. They made you stick out like a botched nose job. I reasoned that the best thing a female cyclist could do to avoid unwanted attention was to wear black and disappear into the cracks in the road. But I discovered that cycling clothes do have an advantage: You always know what to put on. You know which clothes need a wash (those). You don't care if the bottom doesn't match the top. They're always the right weight for the prevailing conditions. They are the clothes you put on clean every morning and rinse the dust and sweat out of with a bit of soap every evening.

On this trip my clothes are a screaming-red Assos jersey with a big white Swiss cross on the back and front, which makes color-dyslexic people think I'm a stretcher bearer with the Red Cross. This is a useful misunderstanding, as I tend to get waved through Third World border crossings with extreme reverence.

The cycling shorts are a necessary evil. They always leave me with a strange tan, a solid line above midthigh separating white from dark—the "Jell-O tan," as it is known in the trade. This "tiramisu look," as I prefer to call it, looks positively awful with a miniskirt and is not recommended, girls.

* * * *

For my Cuba trip I made a decision to use two ordinary waterproof bicycle bags called panniers rather than towing my bicycle trailer, the latter being too conspicuous for someone who might fantasize that it is stuffed with wads of $100 bills, just like in the movies. As usual, I put my sleeping bag, sleeping mat, and stove in the right-hand bag; my clothes, toiletries, and oddments in the left-hand bag; the tent on the rack between them; and the maps in the front bag. I squeeze what few food items I have into the remaining spaces.

I always leave a space in the top of the left-hand bag for my midmorning snack. Maruca loans me a lunch box, a round plastic container with a lid that comes in a mile-high set like a Russian doll. It holds exactly three bread rolls stuffed with bananas and jam, or a very decent refill of rice and beans.

She insists on escorting me down the street to the nearest *campismo* office to make sure I have secured accommodations at my first destination, Mariel. The Cuban idea of camping is nothing so unthinkably dangerous as a thin nylon sheet stretched between two or three metal sticks, but is instead a little concrete cabin with a bed and shower and lockable door, where the annual vacation may be enjoyed in complete safety. *Campismos* are dotted around the countryside, and each year waves of workers are systematically rotated on their week off through these very modest resorts.

The gum-chewing *muchacha* behind the counter in the brochureless and posterless office seems to be well uninformed, as if merely brought in from the burger joint next door to water the plants.

"Is there anything I should do in advance?" I ask.

She inspects her nails and advises me to simply turn up at the *campismo* and see what they say.

Finally, at 10:30 A.M. I bid Maruca "See ya later," squeeze my loaded bike into the elevator, reach ground level, then wobble my way out the front door and up the road.

The first few blocks of my bicycle tours always start this way, like a toddler learning to walk under the lolling load of his large head. The extra precautions I have taken with the economic austerity of Cuba in mind have added significant weight to my load: I have two bottles of stove fuel rather than one, half a cabbage (which keeps well when touring), a two-liter water bag full of certifiably potable water, and enough matches to make an arsonist weep. I head west toward Miramar again and find the little bridge that cyclists and pedestrians are meant to use to cross the busy road.

I locate Avenida 5, a long, straight, empty road leading all the way along the coast of the Florida Straits. The road is bordered by flat coastal farmland that could be anywhere, except for a line of palm trees dotted along the ridge, which informs me that I am in the tropics. The land between me and the sea is filled with large sprouty things, poking out of the ground like the tufts of giant pineapples. I stop to ask a *campesino* (farmer) what they are, and he scrawls in barely legible writing *"henequen"*—an agave plant that, he says, is for making a very strong rope.

About 20 kilometers down the road, I stop to inspect a resort called Villas Cocomar on Playa Salado. The guidebooks tout it. It is deserted though well set up for foreigners, with manicured grounds and a walkway over a gushing stream. I locate the manager holed up in a little booth. He tells me that the price is $36 a single and no, I cannot pitch my tent on that juicy lawn. I know I had better keep on rolling.

I pedal past striking billboards and reassuring messages painted full length on the walls of buildings and factories, messages like 21 MILLION CHILDREN DIE OF CURABLE DISEASES— NONE OF THEM ARE CUBAN!

• • • •

Around dusk I make it to the outskirts of Mariel, proud home of Cuba's biggest cement factory. I crest the rise, and the horizon suddenly morphs into a kind of Dante's hell, an ugly, menacing skyline of chimneys belching gray-green candyfloss against the late-afternoon sky. I coast into the foreground of this unsettling postcard and pedal furiously along the winding narrow road, wanting this vista to improve any minute now. I pass dilapidated factories and tenement blocks, their massive walls stained and perforated by gaping holes, from which the occasional hollow shouts of children escape. A disquieting hum resonates in the sulphurous air, and I have to forcibly clear my nostrils several times of the burning, stinking fumes. I keep eyeing front gardens for a suitable place to pitch my tent, but nothing with a panoramic view of these smoke stacks seems comforting. After a seemingly endless 5 or 6 kilometers, I finally enter the town proper, where the factories, thankfully, give way to rows of small, neat houses and little stores.

I head straight for Hotel Puntilla, a peso hotel on the water's edge. The tariff, 21.80 Cuban pesos (about $1.00 a night), puts it squarely in the Hilton Elite class for Cubans. It is extremely basic, with three floors of unpainted concrete cubicles, each with an open lead pipe for a cold, cold shower. The rooms face the sea, but for some dumbfounding reason, that side of the entire building is a solid, windowless wall. The window in my room instead faces the bare concrete car park and a sad-looking restaurant that I initially mistake for public toilets. I stand in my chosen room and gaze up at the brick wall sealing out the million-peso view and wonder what on earth was going on in the architect's head.

Feeling hungry and ever eager to support local enterprise, I book a table in the restaurant, where I am the sole diner.

The menu lists omelets for 1.95 pesos, *congris* (rice and beans) for 1 peso, and, if I really want to splurge, steak for 2.10 pesos. That's about 9 cents, 5 cents, and 10 cents, respectively. I choose the egg with *congris*. My plate arrives without the beans, so the bill is generously reduced by 0.2 of a peso.

While waiting for my food to arrive, I ask to use the toilet, which, like many toilets in Cuba, does not flush and does not have paper. As always, I carry a tissue wad in my back pocket, but I feel guilty about having to dispose of it in the kitchen bin. I am told that Cubans simply wash themselves with soap and water like the French, sans the gold-fauceted bidet. I usually carry a small cake of soap in a pill box in my pocket, but for some reason I have left it in the handlebar bag on my bike. When I ask if I might wash my hands, I am led into the cavernous kitchen, where Barbara, my congenial hostess, fills a teacup and slowly tips it so I can rub my fingers under the stream. I sheepishly reiterate my request for soap, and there is a scramble to locate the only cake in the building. I look at the stack of unwashed plates on the concrete washstand, the flooded floor, and wonder if I am about to commit gastronomic suicide.

Being the only guest, I am the center of attention. The conversation immediately swings around to how hard Cubans work for so little pay, and the lack of *comida,* or food. This is graphically illustrated by the hand gestures Latinos are famous for: the forefinger wiped across the forehead (hard work), the thumb and forefingers rubbing together (money), and the fingers tapping the lips (food). I am shown a *libreta,* or ration book, issued to every Cuban man, woman, and child at the start of each year. This little brown passport metes out food, soap, and cigarette allowances at extremely nominal prices. Each day of the year Cubans go to their local *bodega,* or warehouse, and collect their allowances. There's a page of thirty-one squares, each square representing a single bread roll, one per person per day. Other pages mete out rice (four pounds a month), beans (four pounds), flour, sugar, margarine, cooking oil, milk (for infants only), meats, even cigarettes (strong or mild). I note that laundry soap is at least separate from personal soap, each person being allowed a small bar of each every six weeks.

"See these shoes?" asks the barman. "Twenty dollars, but you can only buy them with dollars."

The dark, stocky man dispensing *refrescos gaseosos,* or soft drinks in cans, is comparatively well dressed. His shirt, belt, jeans—in fact, everything higher than subsistence level, it seems—cannot be bought with mere pesos. He, like many people I will meet, has access to the magic dollar, either through family living in the States or *trabajo particular,* that is, private, usually illegal, work.

Barbara invites me to go to her mother's house for a hot shower since my hotel has only stone-cold water and tonight there is a chill in the air sweeping across that unviewable water view. I walk with her a couple of blocks to the house, and we talk. She is around forty, divorced with two children, now living with her mother and aunt. A young man suddenly appears at her side, and they exchange words but don't touch—a strange banter. He disappears just as quickly. She tells me that he is her boyfriend and rolls her eyes. A young man at play, appearing and disappearing on a woman in need of companionship.

• • • •

Barbara's family members regard me from their rocking chairs and tell me that I am the first foreigner to have entered their home. The hot shower turns out to be a bucket of water heated over a wood stove. Her mother asks me all about my home country, Australia, and then invites me back to their house when next I pass by, which will probably be a long time from now. I walk back to the hotel escorted by Barbara. On the way I buy her a pot of excellent ice cream for $1.00 from a dollar trailer.

Back in my concrete holiday cubicle, I prepare for bed with some concerns about large spiders crawling through the holes in the flywire. I place my sleeping bag on top of the dubiously clean sheet and then inflate my camping mat and place it underneath as well for double protection against what might be lurking deep in the mattress. I start my evening meditation, sitting cross-legged and propped up against pillows.

After about ten minutes my cosmic connection is disturbed by the rhythmic squeak of well-worn springs and female gasping and moaning in sync. I can tell by the speed of the squeaking and the monotony of the gasping that it is lousy sex, that he is going to come first, she isn't, et cetera. Fascinated rather than titillated, I press my ear up against the wall to verify my hypothesis. A sudden cessation of the gasping and squeaking proves my point. I also predict, correctly, that this tedious ritual will be repeated squeak for squeak at least twice more that evening and once in the morning.

Despite the sleep-shattering sex channel playing live in the room next door, I sleep deeply and unshakeably until 9:30 A.M.

• • • •

I prepare my midmorning snack, three bread rolls bought a couple of days ago in Havana and stuffed with a banana that has somehow stayed unsquashed. Unaccustomed as I am to the rhythm of bike travel after sitting in a swivel chair in front of a computer for months, I do not get on the bike until 11:00 A.M., which is a very late start on a touring day. A late start ultimately screws things up toward the end of the day, when you find yourself stuck in the middle of nowhere with the sun going down, being eaten by mites at dusk, pitching a tent in the dark.

I decide to head 56 kilometers down the road to Bahía Honda, a romantic-sounding destination because it has the word bay in it, which immediately suffuses my mind with swaying palm trees and turquoise water lapping against a gentle crescent of sugary white sand and a cloudless sky. From Mariel

I start climbing up and along a ridge where the views are spectacular: a complex tapestry of craggy mountains, gentle hills, watery pools, and dark swaths of pine trees. I stop at a tiny shop to see if I can buy bread. The shop turns out to be a *bodega,* where Cubans collect their rations and have them marked off in their *libretas.*

Unfortunately, each and every one of its bread rolls is spoken for, and there are no more to sell, even if they were allowed to sell them. A woman collecting her ration at the *bodega* insists that I take one of her two bread rolls; no amount of protesting or pesos can make her change her mind. The generosity of the average Cuban astounds me daily. I thank the woman and pedal off, my loaded bike groaning under the weight, and the love, of the extra bread roll.

About 30 kilometers from Bahía Honda, a government truck, distinguished by its white plate with brown lettering, toots and motions for me to throw my bike on the back. Because I had left my concrete cubicle so late, I do not hesitate to accept the ride. This particular truck is doing the rounds of the local *bodegas,* distributing the day's rations. My bike is hoisted into the back by strong hands, onto the sacks of carefully measured bread, rice, and beans.

I squeeze in the front with the three cheery *trabajadores.* Most Cubans I meet are like these three workers, industrious and committed to their jobs, their frail livelihoods. If the topic of conversation gets around to their economic situation, which it almost always does, they simply shrug. It is the first of many rides I am offered during my journey.

Despite the many thousands of kilometers of fairly flat road, Cubans do not think to tour their country by bicycle. They find it strange that cycle-touring foreigners who have money to pay for a comfortable, air-conditioned tourist taxi or bus would choose to expend so much sweat. Then again, bicycles in Cuba are generally rusting single-speed clunkers with back-pedal brakes oiled by pig fat.

Yet I meet several locals who can cover the distance I've toiled across for two days in only half a day, just to have a coffee with a relative. Bicycle touring is a luxury few Cubans can afford in time or money since overnight accommodations are as expensive for them as for any of us, and despite their meager earnings, no Cuban would dream of sleeping in a tent. *"Peligroso"* (dangerous), they say of their fellow countrymen, making a slitting action with a forefinger across the throat.

· · · ·

The driver refuses my donation of a few pesos, an honorable stance that I discover is rapidly disappearing in the scramble for dollars. Until recently, Cubans were not allowed to possess dollars, so those without family overseas could only stare wistfully at the mobile trailers, parked in every small village, that vend shampoo, underwear, and other mundane goods for dollars, and only dollars.

Perhaps due to the huge numbers of Cubans lucky enough to have those overseas connections, the government opened little currency exchange booths in every village where the people can change pesos for dollars. Officially, the exchange rate is 1 peso per dollar, but in practice this poor rate seems to be applied only to certain government utilities, like train travel. A train ticket costing a Cuban, say, 27 pesos ($1.35) costs a foreigner $27.

The remaining 16 or so kilometers to Bahía Honda are slow

and hot. By late afternoon I roll down the unremarkable main street. My romantic vision of this bayside village evaporates like a snowflake in a hot wok. The bay is nowhere to be seen, and I am suddenly swooped upon by both giant mosquitoes and Cuban room touts looking to make a giant killing.

The village is set about 4 kilometers back from the water, which explains the breezeless, sultry air and a soupy haze of suspended grit. The first tout comes in from the right, a man who leaps in front of my bike, grabs both handlebars, and turns them toward his little house complete with six pairs of eyes staring out from its cavities.

"Fifteen dollars a night," he implores in Spanish. "Shower, rice, beans, eggs, drink." He rubs his stomach in large circles to emphasize the value of the deal, knowing full well how to hook a hungry, tired, and load-bearing cyclist.

From the left I am assailed by an English-speaking tout, who says quietly and mysteriously that he knows of a "really good" *casa particular* with a license—he emphasizes that point loudly to the assailant on my right, where my handlebars are still pointing—for just $10 a night.

The English speaker is Gualberto, a stocky young man around twenty-five years old who teaches the tourist tongue in a local school. His little private enterprise, touting, is probably the most common job in Cuba. The choreography is simple: Approach tourists, show them to a *casa particular,* and then, if it meets the tourists' requirements, collect $3.00 to $5.00 per night for your spotting prowess.

A police car rolls slowly past. The occupants mutter something to Gualberto and then continue on their way.

"See those guys?" asks Gualberto when they are out of ear-shot. "They don't like me talking to you. I never understand it."

He gives me the address of the *casa* and tells me to go check it out for myself. My intention is to check out the hotel listed in the guidebook, but Gualberto insists that it's over the hill and far away. The sun is sinking, the mosquitoes are feasting. I head for the house of Paula and Manolo, tucked away in a muddy back lane.

Gualberto does not disappoint. The house is indeed nice, a cheery two-story clapboard cabin in good condition. This suggests that either business is good or the owners have overseas connections, and judging by the poor tourist appeal of this town, I deduce the latter.

Paula comes out to see what the commotion is. She is a large woman with a smiling and gentle face, and I like her instantly. I negotiate $10 a night, including a meatless breakfast and dinner, and she agrees.

The bedroom is upstairs and would put any decent $60 bed-and-breakfast outside Cuba to shame. It is a large, wood-floored room with a huge double bed covered with a floral bedspread and mosquito net, plus a dresser and ceiling fan. The only marring factor is the cloud of killer mosquitoes, which seem to pass directly through the walls. The shower looks immaculate but does not actually work, so Paula heats a bucket of water for me on the stove, and I do the tin-cup wash in the shower stall for the second day in a row.

I then sit down to the best meal I have eaten in Cuba to date: rice and beans, boiled eggs, chicken and pork cooked in a rich sauce, white rice and warm cheese, and a jug of freshly squeezed orange juice. I am mindful that I had stipulated no meat, which I generally do when traveling to minimize the number of potentially disagreeable germs bombarding my physical body, and to save money. In Cuba there's an added reason: Meat is an expensive luxury here, and I'd feel like I were swallowing their Sunday roast whole and leaving the potatoes. But I long to taste that delicious-smelling chicken and pork dish a few inches from my fork.

Paula is unconcerned about our verbal contract. "Eat!" she insists. I eat just the tiniest piece and insist that her husband, Manolo, take the rest. The flavors of this otherwise unremarkable meal suggest that Paula simply knows how to cook, a rare skill the world over.

Over dinner I learn that six months ago the family's only son escaped to Florida on a small boat. Unlike many who never make it to the far shore, let alone strike it rich in a new country, he is prospering like crazy. They show me pictures of his sapphire-blue Toyota Celica parked in its perfect all-American concrete driveway, and other pictures with members of his new family in an all-American timber kitchen with oodles of cupboards and electrical appliances in the background. Understandably, the family is at once happy and sad for their son. Happy for his success and sad that they may never see him in the flesh again, although they are relatively well off due to his frequent money transfers.

• • • •

Even sadder is Natalia, the longtime girlfriend he left behind, a very pretty twenty-six-year-old who, like 99 percent of her countryfolk, has no way to leave Cuba legally. Natalia works as a dental assistant for Ramírez, a very handsome friend of the family who pops by after dinner to say hello.

Ramírez earns 400 street pesos a month, or $20. This makes him one of the well-heeled professionals in Cuban society. He earns extra money, in dollars, selling clothes. I also meet another friend of the family, a young hairdresser who earns 3 pesos a cut in the hours for which she is licensed, but who makes that money on the sly if clients go to her house. Again, the conversation centers around how little money and food there is in Cuba—yet there is often ample Caribbean lobster to burn.

Paula opens the refrigerator and shows me a plate of fresh, succulent lobster meat that she bought for less than a dollar. This is *langosta escondida,* literally "hidden" or "under the table" lobster. It can legally be served only in tourist restaurants; the remainder is exported. With a twinkle in her eye, Paula explains that if the police were to put their head through the window and see her seafood stash . . . She slaps a hand around her wrist, the Cuban sign for handcuffs.

At some point during dinner I witness *la novela* mania again. The conversation halts midsentence, the diners abruptly evacuate the room, and the TV crackles to life. I decide that when in Cuba, I will do as Cubans do, except endure *la novela.* I retire to my bedroom to write and notice how the television is turned up to near-deafening level, such that I might as well go hunker down there with the rest of them. But I don't.

The next morning I rise early and ask if it is possible to acquire some bread rolls from the *bodega* to refuel my little lunch box. I have discovered an unexpected gastronomic delight in Cuba. The standard-issue bread rolls are absolutely delicious: heavy and moist, with the unmistakable flavor of quality, gluten-rich wholemeal flour. Perfect for pressing a banana into.

Paula is not confident, as there has not been a regular supply of these rolls for days—something about the local mill running out of flour. But she goes out at 6:00 A.M. and returns with seven rolls she has bought on the black market for 5 pesos. From the *bodega* they would have been ten for a peso. She then insists on adding three from the family reserve. Thus, I end up with ten freshly baked rolls. I give the family 7 pesos, or 35 cents, which includes a couple of pesos for their trouble.

Now, you may be thinking: Is this possibly the cheapest, stingiest traveler ever? I can only explain it as a strange and illogical transformation that takes place when a cyclist throws her leg over a loaded bicycle and pedals down a road. That transformation is magnified hundredfold on entering a strange country, especially a poor one. Suddenly, I regress to a clawing, gobbling, sniveling beast of burden. All the poise, padding, and political correctness of my former life is shucked away. I descend down the food chain and become a bicycle-riding ferret with beady eyes and long teeth. Each day I am subject to the elements—splattered by rain, roasted by sun, buffeted by wind. There is no electric window or air conditioner or blow heater to regulate that constant assault on my pathetic little tenth-of-a-horsepower engine straining to make it up an even littler hill. I'm a land-dwelling piranha, snapping at every available caloric opportunity, and sometimes I don't care that the food might be suspect.

When I push on my accelerator on a steep hill, I feel a sensation far removed from that of an air-cushioned shoe sole reflexively depressing a gas pedal in a car. I become a grunting gypsy: moving, eating, sleeping, moving, eating, sleeping. It just so happens that many cultures live close to this level of survival without ever having the luxury of choosing it. But I have the power to choose, and I do. And because I'm expending as much sweat as a *campesino* cutting a hundred hectares of cane with a machete, I believe I am one of them. Can't you see I'm living on the edge here, dammit? I deserve, and I get, respect. And I don't want to pay a cent too much for all that suffering, because that would make me a squishy-soled, voucher-toting tourist. And besides, it might ruin things for the next cyclist who comes along. So, yes, I give Paula and Manolo 35 cents for their trouble, and it all makes sense to me.

••••

The next day I make sure that breakfast is a very simple affair. I cause a minor sensation in the kitchen when I ask Paula to put one of my bananas inside a bread roll so she can toast it over the fire in a pair of waffle tongs. I discover that Cubans are not too adventurous when it comes to food or travel. It seems that the lack of opportunity to extend oneself physically, economically, or creatively has a capping effect on self-expression. They exist in survival mode. There is little energy left over to indulge in fanciful experiments with bananas in waffle-tonged bread rolls.

After breakfast I am filled with indecision about where I should spend New Year's Eve 2000. Do I backtrack 4 kilometers and climb 20 kilometers to Soroa, a mountain village? Do I head for La Palma, 51 kilometers farther on? Do I try to get a ride part of the way to that town, then beat it up the mountain to Viñales, one of Cuba's tourist meccas, some 80 hilly kilometers away?

As it turns out, I do none of those things, which in itself is a good thing. "Plan a holiday, and you'll get the holiday you planned" is a quote I like to think I came up with, though someone with a name like Thoreau or Kerouac probably beat me to it. The only time I heard someone respond, "That's good. You don't want anything unplanned to happen, do you, now?" was in England.

I bid farewell to Paula and Manolo and also to Gualberto, who has turned up to collect his $3.00 tout's fee. Mindful of this, I give Paula an extra dollar to help offset his commission. Gualberto asks me to send him an English-Spanish dictionary. They all wave me farewell from the front porch.

I head toward La Palma and meet a thin, black local called Matalo pedaling his rusty clunker along the road. I ask him to recommend a place to visit, and he speaks highly of La Altura, a beachside *campismo* a mere 15 kilometers down the road, where a cozy cabin costs just 8 pesos a night, or 40 cents. *"¡Playa linda!"* he enthuses and tells me how he worked there as a groundsman last summer. I've ridden 24 kilometers today, hardly enough to raise an eyebrow, let alone a sweat. I suddenly decide that La Altura is as good a place as any to see in the new millennium.

4

MILLENNIUM BUGS

The beaches of La Altura are a mere 12 kilometers away along a remote track, a crank turn in cyclist's terms, yet Matalo insists that he will show me the way. My internal air-raid siren wants to bleat mayday at this offer, but the weather-beaten cane cutter seems harmless and genuinely interested in helping this *turista*. There is something to be said for Latino machismo. They'll not ignore a woman in a pickle.

We reach the crossroads to La Altura, which turns toward *la frontera* (border). Just 145 kilometers (90 American miles) across the turquoise sea is Dollarland.

The paved lane turns into a gravelly bone-shaker hemmed in on both sides by green walls of sugarcane. We stop to pick *guayabas* (guavas) off a roadside tree. The sweet fruit is figlike, only with a tougher outer skin. Farther on we stop at a farmhouse to borrow a machete. Matalo goes into a field and hacks off several lengths of cane, stripping off the bamboolike casing so we can chew on the fibrous stalk. It releases a mildly sweet juice that is addictive under the sweltering mid-afternoon sun.

The road ends at an abandoned airstrip. The runway looks

like a lonely road to nowhere, with giant pieces of scrap iron scattered all over to stop anyone landing on it, creating an unsettling Dalí-esque landscape. The track resumes on the other side of the airstrip, and soon we emerge into a clearing with a cluster of concrete cubicles. *Campismo La Altura.*

This is a Cubans-only resort. I employ every wily feminine ruse in the book (a slender volume on my shelf) but cannot persuade the rule-abiding *jefe* to rent me a cabin, or to let me pitch my tent on the grounds and use the facilities. "We are not authorized to cater to tourists," he says. "It is the rules."

Matalo argues on my behalf, clearly distressed at his former boss's recalcitrance, but to no avail. I sense some friction between the men, as if Matalo's allegiance to this *chinita turista* (pint-size Chinese tourist) is unseemly. When *el jefe* shows no signs of softening, I decide to head through the scrub and onto the beach to look for a place to camp. *El jefe* is not too happy about that, either. Clearly, he does not want to be held responsible for any mishap that might befall this dollar-wielding tourist.

The remote and beautiful beach turns out to be a highly sensitive military zone, heavily guarded by young boys in green fatigues who watch for anyone who might get the urge to set off on a Sunday sail to Florida or, conversely, for a surprise from Uncle Sam to come bobbing over the horizon.

A shady tract of fir trees lining the shore offers the camper's equivalent of a feather mattress: a cushy bed of pine needles. However, not wanting to be wakened by infrared searchlights and the mouth of an AK-47 up my nostril, I push my bike a few hundred meters up the beach to seek permission from the guardhouse perched on the rocky point.

The lone occupant is a gum-chewing teenage boy in full battle dress. He radios his superior after Matalo and I appeal to his un-uniformed streak. The barking reply comes across loud and clear: "NO!"

The reason given is something about military exercises that will be performed on the beach throughout the end of year. The young border guard shrugs, chewing his cud. There is nothing he can do. I decide that I have made all possible attempts to do the right thing and will pitch my tent anyway. If worse comes to worst, a Cuban jail will make a unique and riveting chapter in my memoirs, if I live to write them. In any case, I hear heaven is supposed to be a pretty neat place. . . .

These kinds of vaguely terminal thoughts drift through my weary head as I trudge back toward the row of pine trees. Suddenly I see a small shack hidden a little way behind the hill on a small rise. I point the bike in that direction and mentally make slight adjustments to my sob story for maximum effect. The shack turns out to be a military outpost occupied by a coast guard family celebrating New Year's Eve on the job.

As I approach, three immaculately uniformed soldiers look up from polishing their rifles. I think of waving the snotty white handkerchief in my pocket, but I need both hands to push the bike through the sand. I decide to tell the complete story about the resolute resort manager, the guards, the police—in fact, the whole frigging lot.

They stare at me for some minutes, continuing to buff their rifles. After some low-decibel discussion, Vadero, the most senior of the three with more stripes on his shirt, decides to overrule the fools on the hill and invites me to pitch the tent in front of the house, where they can keep an eye on me. His wife, Adelpha, offers to let me sleep in the house instead, but one look at the dilapidated state of the ceiling and the bug-eaten bed, and I graciously decline.

I give my stoic guide Matalo a dollar for his troubles and bid him farewell. He refuses to accept the money at first, a very honorable trait I am experiencing time and time again in Cuba. A Cuban will not accept money as payment for what he considers *amistad,* or friendship. Only if you say it is *un regalo* (a gift) for his or her child will he or she accept it. Matalo promises to return the following night with a guitar for me to play and pedals off. It is the last I see of him.

· · · ·

I change into my swimsuit inside the tent to avoid the curious, prying eyes of the family's niece and nephew, who have never seen a person disappear into such a tiny room. "Is she going to come out of the *cabañita* (little cabin)?" the little boy repeatedly asks Adelpha.

I oblige, bow to my audience, and then climb down the grassy embankment and wade into the sea. The guardhouse disappears from view. I stare out toward Florida. There's a lot of water in between. The gentle curve of beach behind me glows white against the dark line of fir trees, completely empty of sun worshippers. It arcs around to another point far away to the east, then another, and then another, perfect little beaches scalloping the coastline all the way back to Havana. The sun starts on its journey toward Australia, and the no-see-ums—microscopic mozzies that seem to burrow into the very pores of your skin— soon become I-feel-ums.

I retreat to the house for a bucket bath. Adelpha makes a fire on the concrete slab of a stove, then pokes the ends of two bare wires through a hole in the wall; this makes a fluorescent bulb sputter to life in the "bathroom." I take out the two lemons I have been toting for a special beauty treat: The young hairdresser in Bahía Honda told me to rinse the juice of lemons on my scalp as an astringent conditioner.

As I trot back to my tent, a bloodcurdling gargling and squealing rises from its south face. I halt flop-jawed at the spectacle of the two younger guards, who have pinned down a large pig and are slitting its throat with a sword.

The poor creature takes an eternity to die. You'd think that if anyone was able to kill a living creature efficiently, it would be a soldier. Arturo, the tall, impeccably spit-polished black guard, tries to hasten the bleeding by kneeling on the pig's belly, its neck a gaping bloody hole. At one point we all assume that the creature is finally dead. Arturo stands up, and suddenly the pig springs to its feet with its gizzards spilling from the hole. The bloody apparition runs pathetically around the yard, like a scene from *Pet Cemetery* meets *The Exorcist* and has Rosemary's baby. If I only had a video camera . . . I would not use it.

• • • •

The family insists that I join them for dinner, despite my protests about having my own cabbage and pasta sauce and penne noodles to boil up on my fuel stove.

They have a hard time accepting this, but they also have no idea how much I love and admire my little stove, a life-sustainer to which I have become profoundly attached. It is a simple aluminum bowl with an even simpler methylated spirit burner. Pour a little meths into the tin, light it, set it under the bowl, wait patiently—very patiently—until the bowl's contents bubble, and then eat. In Cuba I have to make do with 70 to 90 percent rubbing alcohol as fuel, which emits a weaker flame that is prone to blowing out at the slightest gust of wind. It requires almost the same persistence as nurturing a wood fire started from rubbing two sticks in an icy windstorm. Incredible that this stove previously fuelled my cycling from one end of Britain to the other over three months, and then my travels in Ireland, Nicaragua, Costa Rica, and now Cuba. I have been seduced by fancier, faster, high-tech models while loitering with intent in camping stores but have never succumbed.

However, I soon learn that in Cuba, it is bad luck to have people eating their own hash in a corner, so I accept the invitation, add my precious half cabbage to the pot, and join their circle.

The meal is a simple affair of rice; black beans simmered with onion, garlic, and oregano that grows wild near the pig shed; boiled yucca; my cabbage shredded with vinegar; and fried pig in *manteca,* or pig fat. Yes, the now-very-dead pig looks humble served in tiny fried chunks in a huge aluminum pot. I nibble a little of the flesh to be polite, but it is tough, the rigor mortis of a bungled execution. I plead indigestion, tiredness, pregnancy—anything to let the ex-pig rest in pieces somewhere other than in my stomach.

We eat from large, oblong platters, army issue, that have several depressions for the different components of the meal. Everything gleams with that unmistakable gloss of pig fat, the cheapest and most reliable source of cooking fat in Cuba—after all, it comes free with every pig. Even the poorest families seem to have a piglet or two snuffling about in the backyard.

Cooking oil, well recognized by Cubans as being "better for the health," costs around $1.50 a bottle and can be bought only in dollar stores, also known as *shopping.* I had ridden past several of these *shoppings* in Havana, each with a long line of patient Cubans waiting to enter Dollarland. My guidebook and several reports say that, as a foreigner with dollars, you can go straight to the front of the queue, and the waves of locals will part like the Red Sea for Moses. But I cannot bring myself to commit such a brazen, classist act.

After the main meal comes the inevitable dessert, a shot of rum. Then *la novela*, this time on a tiny black-and-white television plugged into the same socket as the sputtering fluorescent light in the bathroom. For an hour the swooshing sea creates a relaxing soundtrack to the adultery, betrayal, and subterfuge emanating from the flickering screen.

When *la novela* ends with the lead characters living unhappily ever after, Vadero brings out a *tres*, a tiny guitar with six strings paired off into three sets of two.

I have never seen such an instrument before, and I spend quite a while trying to tell them, in rudimentary Spanish, that there is something wrong with this "guitar." My Spanish is so bad that they do not tell me I am talking a crock of codswallop. My ignorance means that the instrument is quite unplayable in my hands, especially with all eyes and military badges turned my way in a state of high expectation. I manage to plunk out the opening riff of "Lucy in the Sky with Diamonds," but that's about it. In Vadero's hands the guitar fares slightly better, sounding like an untuned ukulele.

The night ends with a swig of *café con leche,* hot milk heated over the fire with sugar and stove-brewed coffee. Many families, including Adelpha's, buy the beans raw, dry them in the sun, and then grind them by hand, swearing that the flavor is superior. It's ironic that the world's hippest cafes are frequented by coffee aficionados whose palates are probably no more exacting than that of the average poor Cuban.

Cuba is where I started, and finished, drinking coffee.

Throughout the evening the no-see-ums step up their own military offensive. Despite nuclear-strength DEET and two pairs of socks, my feet feel as if I have stepped into a puddle of pancake syrup and, from there, onto a red-ant nest. I am literally stamping like a Cossack with a cause as I talk to my hosts.

The Cubans, on the other hand, do not seem to be affected at all.

"They like Chinese food," quips Vadero.

Unable to stand it a moment longer, I bid the family a premature goodnight, again declining Adelpha's concerned pleas for me to sleep in the house under the crumbling ceiling, and make a dash for my tent. Thus sealed inside, and having wiped the tent zipper with DEET to discourage pests from break and entry, the last sound I hear before I turn out the light is Vadero's halting *tres*, backed by the roar of the Florida Straits marching to meet the guarded *frontera* of Cuba.

• • • •

I ask Adelpha where the toilet is, and she looks horrified. *"¡Un hueco!"* she exclaims. It's a hole in the ground.

She motions for me to follow her to an empty house nearby reserved for military visitors of rank and standing. Inside are a dining table and chairs, sofas, a large color television, and a modern bathroom. She waits outside while I hover above the seatless flushing wonder, telling me that neither she nor her family are allowed to use this facility. Instead, they use the hole in the ground near the pigpen.

Cubans have a belief that all foreigners, being richer than even the most distinguished of their fellow countrymen, require a certain standard of appointments when traveling. Thus, it was explained to me that *el jefe* at La Altura *campismo* did not refuse me on racist, sexist, or otherist grounds, but simply because he did not, in the eyes of the authorities, have the standard of facilities befitting a foreigner, especially a single female foreigner. Or else he simply did not want a foreigner to have any opportunity to mingle with ordinary Cubans and paint them too rosy a picture of life outside.

The day is cloudless and sunny. The sea waters of La Altura lap the shore, and there is not a soul on the sand for as far as my eyes can see. It is too beautiful to experience alone, yet too exquisite to share.

I walk for a long time, from one gentle beach to the next. Eventually I come across a thatched shelter. The sandy floor is crisscrossed by the star-shaped footprint of a seabird. Directly in front of this hut, the water stretches out with raised patches of sea grass wafting just below the surface, making it possible to literally walk on water right out into the ocean. In between the warm sea-grass podiums are sandy pools of lukewarm water. I spend a good deal of time hopping from one platform to another, then plunging from one pool to another like a carefree walking carp. Eventually I spot two tiny figures walking along the beach to the hut.

Julio and André are two coast guards doing their rounds. They warn me about *cocodrilos* in the nearby estuary. The three of us gaze out on this perfect sea, and Julio tells me about an Australian asthmatic named Susie who swam across the Straits from Havana to Florida, then followed this feat with several other megaswims. I listen, feeling as though I should have heard of her, just as every Cuban knows about Elián and his unintended megaswim. I've been away from Australia for three years, and I've stopped reading newspapers because they depress me.

I continue walking until I reach the river and a sandbank. Suddenly I spot a perfect pink conch shell sitting in the sand. I set my camera on its tripod to record the find, the time, the place: 9:00 A.M., 31 December 1999, Playa La Altura, Cuba.

Right now I could be at a number of alternate locations offered to me leading up to this date. At a party with Olaf and a seething throng in New York; eating Christmas tamales with Luz Marina García's family in Nicaragua; bantering on the beach with Andréas and Kayak Boy at Playa El Coco, Costa Rica; eating fried breadfruit with Rebecca and Rigo in Bocas del Toro, Panama; or even ruminating alone in my monastic flat in San José, Costa Rica.

But I am here on this beach, alone save for a couple of passing strangers, on the last strand between Cuba and the United States, and I know that I am exactly where I should be. I started out like any other traveler who has not shouldered her backpack for a while: destination-oriented, *I must get to X by tonight.* But I am getting into the rhythm of travel again. Yesterday, I woke with three urgent destinations in my head, and I was stuck in place.

Now, without intent, I am moving.

5

LAND OF THE *MOGOTE*

As beautiful as La Altura is, the no-see-ums are so fixated on my ankles that I cannot imagine another night of possessed tap dancing. It is time to get up and git. This being the first day of the new millennium, it seems a perfect day for change.

Adelpha packs my little plastic container full of *congris,* and I manage to persuade her to keep the two big hunks of ex-pig for her family. By coincidence I learn that she is an aunt of Manolo, from the family I stayed with in Bahía Honda. Adelpha and company wave me farewell through a window, six smiling faces and several arms poking through a single square hole in the clapboard shack. I pedal back along the track to the turnoff, to look again for those *guayaba* trees. But everything appears different now. My stomach is lined with two bread rolls stuffed with banana, which are already wearing off.

Around 1:00 P.M. I turn into the track leading to a hotel called La Mulata, which looks like a pleasant place to buy a juice and eat my *congris*. The hotel is really just an upscale *campismo* dramatically perched on the slope of a steep hill that sheers down to sea level. I encounter an entirely different reception here. The cheery *jefe* tells me that I can pitch my tent "wherever you like," motioning with his hand across the sweeping grounds. The place is empty, save the ample number of staff. In the thatch-roofed bar I buy two *toronja* (grapefruit) juices and two coconut juices for 110 centavos. I later learn that I should ask, "Is that *centavos cubanos* or *centavos divisos?*" The difference is substantial: 110 *centavos cubanos* is 1.1 pesos, or just over 5 cents; 110 *centavos divisos* is 110 cents, or $1.10. Thus, as a foreigner, I was automatically charged twenty times more than a Cuban.

All of the people I meet seem related to one another in some way, and I receive many invitations to stay at their houses *sin interés,* meaning without an expectation that I will whip out my purse on departure. Clearly, the average Cuban is aware of his fellow countryman's tendency to besiege foreigners with requests for medical supplies, gifts, money, and marriage. A foreigner is a conduit to the outside world, and a gift is welcomed like a prohibited substance slipped by sleight of hand through the bars of a prison cell.

I chat with José, a *campesino* who works the grounds and speaks fluent German. He remarks that several years ago Cubans had the opportunity to travel to politically aligned nations such as East Germany, Bulgaria, and Russia, learning and assisting their Leninist and Marxist brethren in arms. Now the travel privileges are a distant memory.

The hotel seems to be run entirely by family and friends of family. I end up hanging out and chatting until late afternoon. Leosymy, a deeply tanned girl with dazzling teeth, invites me to stay at her house in La Palma, just 27 kilometers from where I started out that morning. I accept, and with Leosymy's obscure address scribbled in my diary and the afternoon sun in my eyes, I set off down the empty two-lane highway toward La Palma.

Around mosquito-fall I arrive at La Palma, a nondescript village save for the fantastic hill formations that ring the valley. I have entered the land of *los mogotes,* bizarre conical limestone hills eroded into surreal shapes by karst action, also known as the erosion of irregular limestone by water, to create fissures and caverns both above and below ground.

It is Friday night. Parties are in full swing all around the village. A woman leads me through twisty lanes to the residences of Leosymy's extended family, a collection of dwellings scattered around hilly dirt trails. The view behind the house is alien: The *mogotes* poke out of the mountains like gigantic French baguettes.

I have beaten Leosymy's *colectivo* truck home, so I am taken to her aunt's place to wait for her. Margarita and Francisco are big, black people who tower over me as they point to the map of Cuba on their wall and fire off questions and laugh uproariously and show very white teeth. They offer me a room for $10 a night, and although I gently make it clear that I am staying with Leosymy, they insist that I take a hot bucket bath and eat a meal. I am seated alone at the dining room table, feeling quite conspicuous as people flutter around me like I am a regular at a snobbish eatery. I am served a variety of little plates; the meal itself is a delicious reinterpretation of what I already know well: *congris,* pork, yucca, tomato slices, and a dessert of grapefruit in syrup topped with a thin slice of cheese. In the other half of the room behind a bookshelf, the television blares *la novela* at an addicted throng.

At 8:00 P.M. Leosymy's *colectivo* bus finally arrives. She and her husband, Joel, take me for a stroll through town. A live salsa band is playing in the square; I see couples whirling about expertly and crazily in the street. Joel grabs me and drags me into the square, and I, too, whirl about, clumsy and self-conscious. We wander slowly back through the darkened streets to the house of Joel's mother, Tatika, and a bed is made up for me. I am hijacked by Marielos, Joel's six-year-old daughter from his previous marriage, an acutely intelligent and dramatic little thing who I can easily see becoming Cuba's president, or at least a famous actress.

"I shall autograph your guidebook," she insists, "and you will remember La Palma." She proceeds to scrawl her name inside the front cover.

That night my sleep is long and full of dreams about golden grapefruits rising behind a mountain range of French baguettes.

• • • •

Something tells me that I am not going to get on the bike today. I am sitting in front of a table set with toasted oil bread, a ham-and-spring-onion omelet, a glass of chilled water, a glass of hot milk from the family cow ruminating out back, and a tiny cup of sweet black Cuban coffee.

Again, I am the lone pampered diner. I feel a little less conspicuous when Joel sits down to eat with me. The family watches my every mouthful, and amidst unusual abundance the conversation again gravitates toward the lack of food and money in Cuba, which makes each mouthful I take progressively harder to swallow. They tell me that the current ration allowance is three eggs per person per month and a small ham sausage once a month.

"So," I ask timidly, with a piece of toast in my throat, "have

I just eaten a person's entire monthly ration?"

They all fall about laughing and say not to worry—they simply purchase extra on the street, at a much higher rate, to make up the weekly shortfall. The food from the *bodega,* I am reminded, is not free, though it is priced extremely low and constitutes only about 10 to 20 percent of a person's needs.

Tatika opens a drawer and takes out an old *libreta* from a previous year, all squares duly marked off, and presents it to me as a souvenir. As I flick through the yellowed pages, I involuntarily flash forward to descendants of this Cuban family gee-whizzing over this curious old relic, explaining to their children how *abuelito* (little old granddad) roughed it and musing about three eggs a month and a half a liter of milk, if you were lucky enough to be an infant. I see them sitting around the table eating a synthetic meal pulled out of a plastic packet and popped into a microwave. I see them backing fat-tired four-wheel-drive vehicles with dark windows out of big shopping-mall parking lots, having done their weekly prowl of shelves groaning with the kind of excess I saw on a brief trip to Miami: peanut butter with cinnamon, peanut butter with apple, peanut butter with cinnamon and apple, half fat, quarter fat, nonfat . . .

This family, however, is more self-sufficient, or perhaps more motivated to raise a sweat than other families I have met so far. They own a cow, chickens, turkeys, pigs, a tobacco farm, and a *frijole* (kidney bean) crop. I watch as Alberto, Joel's tough old dad, slowly pours the just-harvested *frijoles* from a large bag while the wind hits the stream of beans at just the right rate of knots to blast away the dust and grit. This very effective sifting process is repeated several times; larger stones have to be sorted by hand. The family even makes its own coarse corn flour for tortillas, crushing the niblets between two granite disks, an eccentrically placed handle somehow rotating the disks against each other with a minimum of human effort.

Leosymy shows me professionally shot photos of her fifteen-year-old daughter, from a previous marriage, at her recent debut. In the photos the daughter is trussed up in a pale blue frilly number reminiscent of Shirley Temple. It's at odds with Cuban simplicity and the sticky weather, but I have noticed this way of dressing girls in other poor societies. It seems like a readily accessible way to express hopes and dreams for your children—hopes and dreams that they will be dealt a better hand in life than you.

Leosymy takes me up a dirt lane to a nearby dwelling. Here lives José, an English-teaching Cuban, with his wife. The fact that his wife is within earshot does not stop him from talking aloud in English about his quest to find that "special woman." The Stephen Stills song that says "If you can't be with the one you love, love the one you're with" springs to mind. José laments that not enough English speakers pass by his patch of dirt. He sits on top of his hill, plunks his guitar, and waits for something that isn't going to show up in a hurry.

Leosymy leaves me with him, saying that she will return in an hour. We watch her disappear over the rise.

"Cubans are very jealous people," José says, cocking his head in her direction. "They like to keep you all to themselves."

"So you think Leosymy objects to me talking to you? Even though it was her idea we meet?"

"Even though."

That evening after dinner, I am invited to watch a video at a neighbor's house, a pirated copy of Bruce Willis in *Last Man Standing* that the neighbor brought back from the Dominican Republic. It is surreal to find myself sitting in a bare-bones shack with a cement floor before a tower of blinking electronics watching a Bruce Willis film. It's an appalling copy, but we all sit riveted to the screen like it's the mother of all *novelas*.

• • • •

Last night I could not sleep for the sound of rave music blasting across the valley. In the morning I go to investigate the source. Perched in a front yard are two huge speaker stacks facing out to the *mogotes*. The speakers dwarf the small house in between.

I walk around with Tatika for almost an hour in search of more bread rolls and some orange-flavored powder to jazz up the water in my drink bottle. The process is prolonged because Tatika stops to greet and kiss on both cheeks every person who comes across her path and because there is no bread, *escondido* or otherwise. We manage to scrounge six rolls, four from the *bodega* at the *libreta* price of 5 *centavos cubanos* each and two from a neighbor who insists that I take them as a gift, pulling out a huge wad of 20-peso notes to prove that he has no need of my dollars.

I pedal towards real *mogote* country and the tourist mecca of Viñales. On the way I stop to inspect a comparatively expensive resort called San Vincente. I use the excuse that I am updating a guidebook, so I get a good look around. While I am admiring the austere concrete pool, a couple of Dutch guys touring in a rental car approach me and ask to hear my story, which is somewhat short at this point in the trip. We agree to meet in Viñales at an address for a *casa particular* that Maruca gave me.

When I arrive in Viñales, I am immediately struck by the tourist-eating ambience, with twee shop facades and cottages. The *casa* that Maruca recommended is indeed beautiful but priced at $30 for a single. No amount of negotiation will have them budge, nor may I pitch my tent in their yard and pay for that privilege, so I decide that this place does not have my name written on the welcome mat.

As I am leaving the Dutch guys roll up and tell me they've found a nice place up the road; they have even explained my situation to the *señora*, who seemed obliging. When I get to Casa Gena, however, it is a different story: She is suspicious of a tourist who cannot afford to pay $30 for a bed and, in any case, if the police were to show up, she would be in big trouble for having an unregistered guest. And no, me eating and paying only for meals would not solve the problem. She motions across the road to another house, and it is the same story over there. No license, *muchos problemas.* I cross the road to investigate anyway. The friendly maid offers her house, which is "not very beautiful," but I can stay for free.

I thank her, thinking that she could probably do with my $10 more than her neighbor on the high side of the street, and I return to the other house to bid the Dutch guys farewell. At that moment the *señora* suddenly changes her mind, perhaps doing a quick calculation of how much one breakfast + one lunch + one dinner possibly multiplied by two days comes to, and says I can camp in her back yard as long as I register my name under the room of the Dutch guys, Willem and David.

I am feeling a little starved for company, and the guys are indeed pleasant company, reminding me of my estranged Dutch lover currently holidaying in the Colombian island of San Andrés with his best buddy.

I cross the road again to thank the maid and explain my new circumstances, then recross the road for the final time. I find a clear patch of dirt between the house and shed to pitch the tent.

This involves moving a few concrete stepping stones and squeezing my tiny tent into the irregular space, which is like trying to force a trapezoidal peg into an elliptical hole. I manage to break a couple of the stepping stones clean in half, making me feel like a right problem guest. Finally, I roll out my mat and sleeping bag and come to rest.

Gena is worthy of her accommodation and meal licenses. Each of us is served an entire fish grilled in tomato-and-onion salsa with potatoes, salad, bread, and a delicious pudding. The meal comes with fresh-squeezed orange juice. This is the best meal I have eaten in Cuba to date.

A license to serve meals in a *casa particular* costs the owner an extra $100 a month, and for this, meals typically range from $3.00 to $5.00 for breakfast, the same for lunch, and $5.00 to $8.00 for dinner. I ask Gena how much dinner and breakfast will cost, so I can balance my blow-outs against my *presupuesto reducido,* or tight budget. She refuses to tell me. The Dutch guys tell me that she said I can pay whatever I want to. Our dinner-table companions are a Canadian father and son who are touring the jazz spots of Cuba together. The son is a sax student at a school in Havana; dad is a *músico* back home. A Ry Cooder and son reprise.

While I am preparing to retire to my tent, Gena's husband comes home, takes one look at the tent, and refuses to let me sleep in it. "No, no, no," he says, shaking a finger at my campsite. As far as I can decipher from his fast Cuban Spanish, he does not like the idea of a woman sleeping out "like this." He thrusts a hand disgustedly in the direction of my nylon castle. The couple insists that I sleep in their own matrimonial bed, and no amount of gracious refusal makes them change their minds. When I notice that they have both gone to bed in the shed, a precariously leaning old shack full of rope and tires and oilcans and a single tatty mattress on a wire base, I realize that to retire defiantly to my tent will be an extreme insult to their generosity, so I decide to dignify the act of giving by receiving.

• • • •

The next day I hang out with my new travel pals. I am thankful for a day to be a passenger and to let someone else do the driving. We go to a cave called El Palenque, notable for its empty, touristy bar out front and equally empty touristy restaurant out back, set on a big, queer meadow ringed by the sheer faces of *mogotes* plunging to the earth from a high place. Mosquitoes are out picnicking, so glad to see us that they drive us back to our car. We continue to Cayo Jutías, a foreigners-only beach about 45 kilometers north. As with many similarly "gated" areas, there is a booth and boom gate a good way back from the actual beach where we pay an entrance fee before being waved through.

Parked at the gate is a taxi with three girls from Ireland inside. The taxi driver is not allowed to pass the gate to bring them in, so they get in the car with us. The day is glaringly bright, the sand is painfully white, and the heat from the sun is such that if you stand still for a minute, you can feel your flesh start to sizzle. We find a spot in the shade just beyond the parking lot. Sure enough, a boy approaches to tell us we cannot park there. We are meant to park in the unshaded official lot, where they can keep an eye on us. I feel in an argumentative mood and make a comment about there being a lot of rules in Cuba.

"¡Muchas!" says the boy, and repeats his boss's request for us to move. We move.

The beach is almost empty, and although the water is fine,

it is a little too warm to be refreshing on such a sweltering afternoon. When hunger strikes and the Pringles run out, we decide to meet at the restaurant farther along the beach.

A band is playing under a thatched shelter, and the backdrop is aqua, indigo, and white: sky, sea, and sand. Here, I let my head go and order a lobster something-or-other for $6.50.

At the table behind I can see three utterly gorgeous Italian guys chatting and eating plate after plate of the same lobster something-or-other that I am eating. I am wearing my mirrored biking glasses, so I feel entirely at ease feasting on both my meal and the object of desire directly facing me. He is matching my stare blink for blink, quite possibly admiring his own reflection. Only later do I discover that the mirror has all but worn off my sunglasses and that he could see my peepers clearly.

"They're after the hookers," says Willem matter-of-factly.

I envy the hooker who reels in this one. Indeed, all over Cuba I see young Cuban *chicas* hanging out with young and old foreign men, and occasionally an older foreign woman playing footsies with a young Cuban man. Women pull out pictures of their *esposos* (husbands), who invariably are in Europe or the States for an extended period, taking care of some business— but yes, they are coming back, maybe next month, for a couple of weeks, and they will bring stuff, like this television set . . .

I meet many Cubans who love their country, yet the desire to escape, to know the outside world, even for five minutes, even for a drink bought by and shared with a foreigner, can be so great that Cuba has become a mecca for those foreigners seeking a Mr. or Miss Right Now. Someone the travelers can enjoy in a tropical part of the world, far away from the prying eyes back home, and then conveniently put into cold storage until the next package vacation or business junket.

• • • •

We return to Viñales via a tortuous and altitudinous back route called Minas de Matahambre, a great way to get lost for the outstanding views of the *mogote*-studded region. At one point we find ourselves wending through the middle of a giant *mogote* thanks to the confusing directions that Willem obtains from a passing local in exchange for a dollar bill.

That night Gena outdoes herself again, serving a huge roast chicken in salsa with all the trimmings. I manage to convince her and her husband that I need to sleep in my tent, feigning spiritual reasons, and they finally shrug and let me be.

I arrange to meet the Dutch guys in Pinar del Río in two days' time in order for them to give me a ride to María La Gorda, a remote diving spot at the far western tip of the country. I prepare to pay the *señora* for two dinners and two breakfasts, which I expect to be on the lower end of the acceptable range. They turn out to be at the extreme upper end for a *casa particular*—that is, about $9.00 for dinner, $6.00 for breakfast, and a staggering $1.00 for every juice. Based on the number of juices I have drunk, thinking they are in the region of 25 to 40 cents, it seems the bill will come to well over $40. Gena asks for $15, and that is that. Because she enjoyed a full house for two days, she probably paid off her monthly licenses in one night and can now relax. (If a *casa particular* cannot pay the fee, its license is revoked, forever.)

The ride to Pinar del Río is an easy climb up a mountain and a swift downhill. Halfway up the mountain, a woman invites me into her cottage; within twenty minutes, lubricated by several sweet homegrown oranges, I am lined up for her guest room and her underage son's hand in marriage.

Pedal pedal.

A little farther on I meet Ben, an Australian advertising copywriter currently based in Cambodia.

Pedal pedal.

I arrive in Pinar and ask for road directions to the houses of Ana and Nieves, the two Cuba members on my Women Welcome Women World Wide (www.womenwelcomewomen .org.uk) membership list. Based in England, this mutual hospitality and friendship club supports traveling women in seventy countries. It makes landing in a strange new place just a little bit more welcoming.

No one seems to know how to get to the street address I have written in my diary. A very old black man on a bicycle takes me to the local radio station where the idea, I think, is that an announcement will be made over the airwaves.

I wander down the road to a juice stand and sit down to wait. At the table is a Cuban girl and a blond guy who tells me that he is from Sweden. He works six months of the year in his chilly home country as a forklift driver and spends the other six months with his Cuban girlfriend. After we exchange four or five sentences, they give me their address and welcome me to come and stay. This kind of open and instant hospitality is becoming even more routine than "Have a nice day" in America or "G'day" in Australia, with a lot more at stake, and I wonder if the Swede and I would be as forthcoming back in our respective home countries. There is something in the air here in Cuba, an air of brotherhood among strangers, something I have not experienced since I backpacked in Asia many years ago.

I return to the radio station in time for Carlos Manuel, a voice actor on the local radio version of *la novela,* to come down and assist me. He's a birdlike man, with eyes and hands full of life and expression. He lives right round the corner from Ana; they've been neighbors for years but have never met until today. It is odd entering a strange new world and becoming a catalyst for new relationships. Ana's house is a big colonial terrace where she and her husband, two kids, mother, and giant Afghan hound live. She works in one of the dollar boutiques selling expensive clothes to tourists and wealthy Cubans.

Ana immediately calls up Nieves, a town planner, and the two women take me around town after dark and point out the rich array of colonial architecture in the main street. I am particularly taken by a kitschy blue-and-white art deco apartment block with curvy balconies and curly railings.

That night we eat *langosta* (Caribbean lobster) in salsa, all *escondida,* of course. I make sure to nibble just a little lobster, but being Cubans, they graciously pile the lobster on my plate like it's rice and beans. *"¡Come, come!"* they say. Eat, eat.

Pinar del Río is the home of the cigar industry, and I go to see the cigar-rolling process at the local factory/museum. Seated in row upon row of small booths are people rolling the tobacco leaves into the various cigar shapes—fat ones, skinny ones, short ones, long ones. The cigars sell in the adjacent shop for as much as $700 a dozen, presented in exquisitely tooled leather cases. Later, Carlos Manuel takes me to an unmarked door in his street where a man makes cigars to sell to locals, at 1 peso each, or 5 cents. I put in an order for twenty-five, thinking that they'll make neat gifts for the diminishing number of smokers in my life, and the even fewer who smoke cigars.

• • • •

At 2:00 P.M. I stand with my bike folded and bags packed and wait for the Dutch guys to show up and give me a ride to María

La Gorda, some 150 kilometers west. As it turns out, they decide not to go that far but instead to stay in Sandino, about 90 kilometers from Pinar del Río.

Sandino is a town with absolutely no redeeming features, except for proximity to some sea coast and a very nice *casa particular* called Motel Alexis. *La señora,* on hearing that I am not going to stay in one of her cozy floral rooms with private flushing toilet, insists that I eat a meal and refuses payment. She fills my lunch box with rice and beans and gives me six apples from her tree. The Dutch guys then give me a ride another 30 kilometers down the road to where they want to turn off to another beach. At the drop-off point we bid each other farewell for the last time. They offload on me a very welcome half bottle of SPF-15 sunscreen and an excellent road atlas of Cuba. Then they are gone.

From here it is an easy 30-kilometer run of flat, flat, flat riding to the peninsula. The road is a single black strip flanked by coastal shrubs. I stop at a roadside table with a single plump papaya for sale for $1.00. Somehow I manage to balance the football-size fruit on the top of my groaning panniers. Food. I have developed an obsession about food ever since I ran out of steam and hit the wall on my first long day trip with a cycling club a few years back. I had packed a large slice of vegetable lasagna and an apple, thinking that would be enough for lunch, but by late afternoon when we were racing to meet the train, I became so weak that I rode with my head slumped on the handlebars. Someone produced a brownie; I recall snatching it from his hand and gobbling almost all of it before he snatched it back. Upon which I think I growled like a dog.

· · · ·

I round a bend, and María La Gorda, Cuba's most isolated, foreigners-only hotel, springs into view. There is a strange silence and sense of space here that tells me I am a long way from anything. The unbelievably clear, blue water nudging the gentle, palm-studded crescent of white beach is marred only by the whirr of a huge electrical generator at the far end that runs day and night. I feel sorry for the 5-peso-a-day guards who live four to a concrete cubicle right beside it. They just shrug and say, "You get used to it."

The hotel is a series of cabins and blocks of differing ages scattered along a sandy path. The tariff, $40 a night, puts it squarely outside my budget. Ditto the dinner buffet at $15. The extra pasta and salsa I have ferried all the way from Havana will now pay off.

I go into reception armed with a letter of introduction written by Ana's husband, who used to work here. The letter asks politely if the management will assist me in finding a safe place to pitch my tent. They point me to the beach directly out front, where they can keep an eye on me. I pitch the tent under the palms as instructed, taking advantage of a nearby light; fortunately, I am as far away from that infernal generator as possible.

As I sit in front of my tent watching the sunset and making a sizeable dent in my papaya, a group of Swedish thirty-or-forty-somethings passes by. They invite me to join them that evening for a *Cuba libre* (rum and cola with a dash of lime) in front of their *cabina*. When party time arrives I zip up my tent and, taking a chance, put my toiletries in a bag with the intention of brazenly asking if I may use their shower. When I get to their cabin I find that they have snaffled a piece of pizza from the buffet for me. It is interesting, and fortuitous, that cyclists bring out a curious mixture of pity, concern, and moderate respect for their suffering in the eyes of the average onlooker; I am often perceived, I think, as an undernourished, unloved vagrant in danger of being ravished, being rained upon, and suffering a flat tire.

I take a seat around the fire, and the group is introduced thus: doctor, doctor, lawyer, banker, orthodontist, insurance salesman, doctor.

"Dropout," I think of responding when it is my turn to fess up, but I bite my tongue. I engage in fairly light conversation with a somewhat pompous orthopedic surgeon who cannot see the point of what I am doing.

One of the group (is it the orthodontist or the lawyer?) allows me to use the shower in his hotel room. As I am washing my sweaty cycling clothes in the sink, I glance around the room and recognize the accoutrements of a nonvagrant: expensive colognes, aftershaves, moisturizers, hair gels, designer underwear and shirts, soft leather Italian shoes, stylish and unscuffed luggage. In my drawstring mesh sack is a toothbrush, toothpaste, dental floss, and a squeeze bottle of all-purpose cleanser that claims to be gentle enough for face, hair, body, clothes . . . pots and pans. I look closely at my face in the shaving mirror and notice that my skin is not as Teflon-smooth as it was the last time I looked.

The professionals retire to their respective rooms and I retire to my tent, hanging my wet clothes on my bike and hoping that they will still be there in the morning. They are.

• • • •

Everything at María La Gorda is expensive. To rent a snorkel, a mask, and fins costs $12. I ask if I can just rent the snorkel and mask.

"Why?" asks the attendant.

"Because I need to save money," I say.

With that he gives all three pieces of equipment to me for nothing, telling me it is the Cuban price and that I may bring them back at the end of the day.

I spend the afternoon paddling about in the amazing, clear water, with huge gardens of coral and plant life looming up from the depths like giant cauliflower. The water is so salty that it is easy to stay afloat and swim far and wide, even without flippers.

I meet three young guys from London who are waiting in reception for a room to come available after spending a night in their car. They all work in advertising and are friends with someone I have worked with in Australia. The world is shrinking by the minute. We are all tanning our pale bodies on the beach when a big, bearded South African sailor named Peter walks up, stops, and points to a tiny vessel bobbing out beyond the dock.

"My boat," he says. "Been 'round the world twice in that little thing. Want to check it out?"

The guys swim; I get into a dinghy. The boat is indeed tiny: a single bed and a table, a couple of gas burners inside a kitchen nook, and that's it. Peter had sailed around the western side of Cuba from Florida, stopping in Havana, where he "bonked" a Cuban girl who "looked like she'd stepped out of *Vogue*." His plan is to continue sailing around the coast to the much-hyped tourist town of Trinidad, some 640 kilometers by road and about a third of the country east, where he will meet up with his babe (and her babe from a previous liaison) and live happily ever after. On the way he will stop at Cayos de San Felipe, a rarely visited cluster of mangrove and sand islands where he hopes to catch some lobster.

Around 5:00 P.M. he stops by my tent and asks if I want a ride—a ride to Trinidad on his boat, that is. He calculates that we should make it in about three or four days.

I think of all the reasons I should decline this interesting offer. I've told Ana and Nieves that I will return to Pinar del Río in a few days to see them. I want to pick up the cigars I have ordered. From there I am going to Isla de la Juventud (the Isle of Youth), a large island off the southern coast of the province. Most importantly, I get boatsick. Peter himself seems a bit boorish, though after four years of traveling, I've developed a tolerance for an ever-widening spectrum of crazies and boors. I open my mouth to politely decline and say, "Sure."

I pack my tent, fold the bike, and with the help of Graham, one of the Brits, load my stuff into Peter's dinghy against the sinking sun. We have to sign some papers with an immigration official. As we pull away from the dock, the entire population of the hotel comes out to wave us off. A Swede named Karl, who is studying saxophone in Havana for a year, says how envious he is that I can just take off like that. The envy is mutual. I hanker for his career-oriented purpose there, with the full support of an uncommonly adventurous dad. He's come from somewhere cozy and is on his way back to same. He's going to have a job he likes and a retirement fund. Wife and kids and all.

Peter and I speed off into the setting sun, toward the small, dark silhouette of the waiting ship, with Graham's camera flashing constantly.

6

THE WORLD'S WORST SAILOR

First mistake: I insist on cooking a meal before we set sail. I reason that it is better to cook a meal in these calm conditions than to juggle pots and pans while the boat is capsizing later. And how calm it is. The sea is a sheet of black glass in which the moon floats without a ripple. The stars are the lights of a celestial big city. The hotel back ashore is identifiable by a couple of glowing dots in the distance. The only thing marring this vision of nocturnal tranquility is the distant yet distinctly audible sound of the generator, whirring, whirring . . .

Peter has placed my two panniers and my tent in plastic bags, warning me they will most certainly get wet otherwise. He wedges my bike under the table, also covering it with plastic. He calculates that if we leave at 7:00 P.M. and sail all night, we should reach Cayos de San Felipe by 10:00 the next morning.

From my panniers I pull out a carrot, a cabbage, a sachet of ready-to-eat tomato salsa, and pasta and throw it all in a pot. The little gas stove in the cooking nook is fast and effective. We wash the one-pot concoction down with a glass of lemon powder mixed with water and later make coffee. We do not set sail until 10:00 P.M. I am sure Graham and company must be staring out from the shore to the small light on top of the mast, looking at their watches and wondering what on earth is going on in the boat. After washing up, Peter sets the engine going and we finally trawl out of the bay, ominously called the Bay of Currents, until the winking lights of the hotel and the whirr of the generator fade into the darkness.

Sometime around midnight the wind picks up, and the boat starts to roll slowly about like a pair of jeans in a tumble dryer.

I am sitting on deck enjoying the night sky when a strange tiredness suddenly comes over me. I start to yawn . . . deep, frequent, and quite uncontrollable yawns.

"Aha, the first sign of seasickness," grunts Peter.

A short while later I make a grab for the bucket and half fill it with the first of several gutfuls of pasta dinner. A few meals-in-reverse later, I top it all off with rice-and-beans-in-reverse from lunchtime.

Peter, meanwhile, is studying the maps, checking the compass, staring at the sky, and looking perturbed. We are, he says, particularly unlucky because the wind is on the nose of the boat all the way.

It gets worse. The tumble dryer soon turns into a ringer washer on neurotic cycle. Because of the wind, 55 nautical miles to Cayos de San Felipe becomes 120 nautical miles, and Peter must tack the boat through the rolling seas every fifteen minutes. This means that I have to move from my sickbed on the bunk to the floor and back again, back and forth with each change in direction, unless I want to be flung bodily between the two locations. I am sucked into a watery underworld, a surreal vortex of fitful sleep and nauseous wakefulness that continues all night, and all the next day. Eventually there is nothing more to piss, poop, or throw up, but, undeterred, my body continues to issue its nightmarish trio of evacuation directives. I cannot even appreciate the spectacular starry night that stretches as far as the eye can see.

•••••

To make matters even worse, Peter insists on chain-smoking a brand of truly foul Cuban cigarette that makes me want to gag in between dry retches. The cigarettes are made from the absolute dregs of the tobacco leaves used for rolling export-quality cigars. In the chaos I notice that he never puts the cigarettes or lighter back in the same place, cursing when he cannot find them in the next two minutes, and soon I am putting things back in retrievable places in between being thrown from bunk to floor.

At 5:00 P.M., seventeen hours after toasting coffee mugs to our impending adventure, the desolate, low-lying mangroves of Cayos de San Felipe bob hesitantly over the horizon. I stare at this chimera of terra firma, drained of all energy save for a few flickering calories to focus my retinas on my bikini top flapping on the railing, then on the island in the background, then back to my bikini in the foreground, as I have been doing in a trance for the past six hours. I am still dry retching periodically as we drop anchor, unable to move or otherwise respond to Peter's light conversation about a large school of bottlenose dolphins leaping and cavorting in the waves beside us.

As we draw closer my eyes grudgingly move in their sockets to scan the beach for a place to pitch my tent.

"You don't have to go to all that trouble," says Peter. "You're more than welcome to sleep in the boat."

I stare at him as a hostage would a kidnapper. I manage to drag myself into the hold, pull out my pannier containing the camping gear, and then throw it in the dinghy. Peter offers me some hot, sweet Cuban coffee with condensed milk, and I sip it delicately. We climb in the dinghy and putter to the shore, my legs crumpling beneath me as I climb out of the boat. The fine white sand squeaks underfoot like icing sugar. Dotted along the beach are large, bleached conch shells, lacy sea fans petrified by the fierce sun, and little else. My captain returns to his ship, and I am alone.

With the earth swaying and the sun sinking, I pitch the tent faster than ever before in my life. I light the mosquito candle and heat the five liters of water I lugged from Pinar del Río for a bath in my tent.

At 8:30 P.M. I crash under the black Cuban sky, now on fire with stars. In the distance Peter's navigational light bobs. Tomorrow we will search for lobster.

● ● ● ●

I wake early, after a night of rolling, crashing, waterlogged dreams. The sun beats down on my tent and turns it into a sauna. In my shattered state last night, I did not study the shade, slope, or wind factors for the optimum tent site. I pitched where I happened to place my foot.

I take a long walk, the sand smooth and devoid of human footfall. There is a remarkable variety of flotsam and jetsam waiting to be picked up by no one: huge shells beached like old shipwrecks, petrified seaweed clumped like discarded mop ends, and more of those intricate sea fan skeletons.

An hour or so later Peter comes roaring across the waters in his dinghy. Also in the bay is a newcomer, a large, impressive yacht. It's the home of a German family on their way around the world, and Peter informs me that he has encountered them several times on his voyage to Cuba. We speed along the beach in the dinghy and enter a waterway that seems to cut through to the middle of the island. The passage opens into a flat, mangrove-filled lagoon. The little lake becomes too shallow and thick with vegetation to get very far in. I look across at my burly sea captain framed against this fantastic backdrop and think, "If only I was in love with him, this would indeed be a picture of paradise."

We back out of the mangroves, and at my request Peter leaves me on the beach to do more combing while he goes off in search of lobster. He returns after an hour ranting furiously about the giant mother of all crustaceans he almost caught and how crappy his spear gun is. His exact words:

"Had him lined up and *pow!* This shit-stick blew it apart."

He holds up the tattered fragments of two crustaceans that clearly had alternative plans for the day until he arrived. I wonder if they are languishing in the same neck of heaven as the pig from La Altura.

We return to the boat. Only hunger permits me to set foot on the Deck of the Damned again to augment our catch with instant mac 'n' cheese from a packet. Although the synthetic sauce mix overpowers the delicate lobster flavor, it's not too bad. We decide to pay the Germans a visit.

The German yacht *SeeWolf* is a vessel to behold. An immaculate craft ten times the size of our little float, it sports the top of the line in everything. Imagine a 007 inflatable dinghy, four bedrooms, a gourmet stainless-steel-and-timber kitchen outfitted with every conceivable convenience, and a proper tiled bathroom with a fluffy mat and toilet-roll doll. The pantry is stocked with food for six months, carefully packed, labeled, and frozen. Baskets of garlic and onions hang gaily from the ceiling. A computer and onboard satellite dish enable the family to surf the net and send and receive e-mail. The dingy looks ready for an international rescue mission at a moment's notice.

Harold and Barbara decided to sell their house and business back home and simply sail off the grid into the sunset. Different members of their family and friends have joined them at various times throughout the journey, which has been going on for two years. They cannot imagine going back to their old landlocked life.

The male contingent decides to board the Bond inflatable and head off to another part of the island. MISSION: LOBSTER. The Germans are outfitted in style, with matching skin-diving gear and lethal sea-hunting knives slipped into purpose-made scabbards in their boots. They drop me off on the beach so I can move my tent to a shadier spot and spend as much time as possible on terra firma. I laze around, and toward the end of the afternoon the impressive inflatable comes roaring over with the catch: seven giant lobsters. So it is back to the German floating villa for flour tortillas with chicken mince, tomato, cucumber, olives, sour cream, cheese fondue sauce, and, of course, grilled lobster, all washed down with delicious iced tea.

I send an e-mail to my Dutch beau in Costa Rica; weeks later I find out that it never arrived.

Although the lobster is delicious, my stomach starts complaining that even this mini ocean liner is not dry land, so the boys return me to my campsite in the inflatable. By now it is dark, and even though we sweep the shore with a powerful, impressive, German-engineered flood lamp, we are astounded at how difficult it is to find my tent. My eyes feel useless, as if staring at life through a black cloth.

"Aren't you scared to be sleeping out there all alone?" asks Stefanie, the twenty-something daughter whose boyfriend has joined her and her family for a six-month sabbatical.

"Well, what's out there that's gonna get me?" I ask.

She shudders.

That night my ears prick up whenever I hear a rustling in the bushes. Fearful people have the knack of planting the most fertile seeds of doubt.

• • • •

Over breakfast Peter tells me that we must spend up to two more days on the island to wait out the weather front that gave us so much hell. From there it will be another two days to Trinidad. Alternatively, he says he can let me off at Isla de la Juventud, the large island off the south coast of the mainland. I am left to ponder this choice.

One consolation is that Peter and the German A-team go out and catch fourteen lobsters. Big ones. We build a fire on the beach near my tent and barbecue the critters in olive oil and lemon juice, accompanied by Barbara's potato salad and more of that delicious iced tea. Stefanie has generously brought her guitar to shore in the dinghy. As the sun sinks I play the song I wrote six months earlier for my Dutch beau, called "Song for Jungle Boy."

Stefanie and her boyfriend stand listening, arm in arm under the starless sky.

Song for Jungle Boy

Lying here beside myself
I feel your breath but it's just the breeze
And the TV's talking but I ain't listening
I'm waking up beside you high in the trees
You don't love me
You don't love me
You don't love me and that's OK
I tell myself
I tell the walls
I tell my guitar every day

Yeah I'm alright yeah I'm OK
You got your life go your way
And I do the things that I gotta do
But in between it all
I think of you

The longing comes and the longing goes
But it never ever really disappears
And I can take the highs and I can take the lows
But every now and then I gotta fight my tears
I see you when my eyes are closed
I see you when they're open wide
Like a vision I can't get you out of my head
And the hunger I feel for you deep inside

Yeah I'm all right yeah etc.

I never want to be a pain
I never want to tie you down
I never want to clip your wings
Or like a shadow follow you 'round
I watch you fly, free as a bird
I watch you disappear a dot in the sky
I watch you 'til you've gone from view
And I dream of when I
Lay close to you.

• • • •

The new day begins gently, well before sunup.

"*The world's worst sailor*—that's what the asshole had the nerve to call me!"

Peter is regaling me with the story of a Dutch backpacker who had hitched a ride on his boat last year. Meanwhile, he is stumbling about in the dark looking alternately for his glasses, his binoculars, his prongy things for measuring distance (called dividers, I think), his cigarettes, and that flat screwdriver.

". . . and I've been around the world *twice* in this thing. *Alone!*"

We are not shipshape. Just out of the bay, the engine suddenly splutters and breaks down, leaving us with nothing but sail power to complete the journey.

After we spend hours bobbing back and forth in a breeze with the knot speed of a baby's breath, the wind picks up as the blue-gray pall of dusk falls all around the boat.

Sometime between January 10 and 13, with the boat thrashing about wildly like a bathtub toy possessed and Peter somewhere out on the bow—stark naked and drenched, yanking ropes and repeatedly cursing whoever might be listening above, "You motherfucking *cunt!*"—I start to concur with the Dutch backpacker.

At some point Isla de la Juventud appears, bounces up and down for an hour, then fades off into the distance. The offer to drop me off there is retracted for reasons of safety, says Peter, given that our engine is dead.

I spend most of this period in a surreal twilight zone, thankfully drugged by some Dramamine I found in a small drawer. The drug keeps the nausea at bay and helps me sleep in between moving from bunk to floor to bunk every time the boat tacks and bailing out the mounting pool of water in the hold. I drift in and out of consciousness, at one moment dreaming about being on a calm sea with no sound, and the next moment slowly waking to find myself in a turgid hell. I don't know which of the two states, dreaming or wakefulness, I am actually in.

When it is my turn to keep watch, I slump on the seat, hand clutching the rail for support, and stare. Peter hauls himself inside now and then, apologizing each time for his nudity, which I haven't much noticed.

The problem is that Peter expected a front to arrive that would carry us speedily to the port of Trinidad in two or three days. The front never arrives. Instead, we endure the worst possible scenario: even stronger headwinds all the way that effectively triple the duration of the voyage.

By day three, with the boat repeatedly flinging itself down in the troughs between waves with a skull-jarring *crack* and swinging about wildly on the crests, I decide that I have had enough and demand, weakly, because I can hardly talk, to be let off as soon as possible. As we have long passed Isla de la Juventud, this will have to be at Cayo Largo, still only half way as the crow flies to Trinidad.

At noon we finally limp into the waters of this foreigners-only resort island. Peter is not happy, cursing about how this detour is stopping him up from getting to Trinidad, how I am keeping him from his Cuban babe, how I am letting down the buddy of Fidel who had lined up some work for Peter, and, to top it off, how impossible it will be to enter the reefy marina with a dead motor.

I somehow find my lips and tongue and suggest weakly that we wave down the passing catamaran and get them to toss us a line. At this, Peter explodes.

"I am the captain of my own boat. How dare you sit there and tell me what to do!"

Shortly thereafter, somebody on the cat tosses us a rope and tows us safely in. Peter starts a new rant about not being able to get out again the following morning. I have the audacity to add that a catamaran or somebody will probably give him a tow out if he asks nicely, but I think this advice is lost on the world's worst sailor.

• • • •

We dock. I crawl onto the pier and hug the planks. A boatload of polo-shirted, loafer-footed tourists glides alongside and spills its bounty onto the dock. The tourists file past, glancing indifferently at my prostrate form and folded bicycle.

A swarm of coast guards and immigration officers descends upon us and proceeds to extract our life histories and possessions. They tell us to open all our bags and spread the contents out on the dock for meticulous examination.

"Are you married?" asks the guard assigned to examine every stitch of my clothes sack. I can tell they think it odd that

Peter and I are sharing a boat but are not romantically entangled. The guard motions to his comrade, who is busy going through the stash of mac 'n' cheese on the boat.

"Jorge is looking for *una novia*," the guardsman says. *Novia*, I learn, translates to "girlfriend" but is actually closer to "fiancée."

Jorge emerges from the hold with Peter's map of Florida, which is maybe about as much as his eyes will ever see of the forbidden land, and grins entreatingly at the bedraggled potential wife before him.

Another official with a clipboard nails Peter for not flying both Cuban and South African flags, apparently an international maritime regulation. He pleads poverty, and eventually I give him $15 toward the $20 flag, the amount I was going to give him for my three-come-five nights of hell anyway. He takes the money without thanking me and triumphantly goes in search of those disgusting Cuban cigarettes.

• • • •

I discover that I have landed in a new predicament. I need just one night to recover, wash the puke off me, and return to sanity. My plan is to ask for the cheapest "stranded maiden" price for a hotel room or, failing that, to ask to rent a staff room or, failing that, to ask permission to pitch my tent in a spot that will not disturb anyone or, failing that . . . well, I fully expect to not fail.

But for the first time in all my days of traveling, I do fail, on all three counts, a point that Peter notes gleefully.

I use every tactic in the Extreme Circumstances Survival Handbook, including pleading, shameless flattery, advanced bribery, hunger striking, and feigned death, but from the expressions of the hotel staff, I might as well be selling a timeshare in Guantánamo Bay.

No matter how pitiful my circumstances, I am still a foreigner. I arrived in a fancy vessel from the land of freedom, where there are more than two channels on the television spectrum and jeans without holes. I am not in any kind of distress that they can detect, not even close to the kind etched in every Cuban's psyche during the hardest years of the U.S. embargo. I am presented with two options: pay $93 for a hotel room (meals and alcoholic drinks included) alongside the Italian, German, and Canadian package tourists or, for $40, leave the island on one of the late-afternoon flights to Havana or Varadero, Cuba's resort epicenter.

I seriously consider the five-star lodging option for a full three and a half minutes. My body aches, my gut aches, my head is still swirling somewhere beneath the waves. I stink to high heaven, and everything I own is wet. Truthfully, I can afford this one night of excess, but one thought runs through my addled head: If I am going to pay that kind of money, do I want to spend it in this "special municipality" where no Cuban is allowed on the premises, except to wipe the tables and swipe the AmExes of foreigners, and where nothing can be done for a damsel in distress? Nope.

I opt for Varadero since a return to Havana goes against the grain of a touring cyclist, moving ever forward, rarely backtracking. Besides, Varadero is the only side of Cuba that many foreigners ever get to see, and I want to see all sides of the melon.

By late afternoon bike and I are airborne, winging away from an exclusive outpost in Cuba's growing inhospitality industry and leaving behind one of the worst case studies in the history of human hitchhiking.

7

CUBA FOR BEGINNERS

The first sign that I am headed for the Riviera of Cuba comes in the form of a little box of reconstituted juice offered to me on the flight from Cayo Largo to the mainland.

"That will be a dollar," says the steward after I empty the contents in one suck.

I board the tiny airplane with a tour group of young Italian funsters who are staying in Varadero, the Cuba that Fidel wants the tourists to see. They are returning from a daytrip to the island where I washed up comatose just five hours before.

I switch into survival mode and sniff out the leader of the pack to see if I can den with someone who might be holidaying solo and open to renting his or her empty second hotel bed.

"Em zorrie," says the bilingual guide, waving his clipboard. "All ziss peoples are in dopples."

Of course they are in *dopples*. Just what am I thinking? Hardly anyone holidays alone in an all-inclusive resort unless they're writing a review on it. I remember the last time I stayed in one and I was not writing a review. I was invited to the wedding of a Spanish friend to a stunning Costa Rican girl, and in true Latino form everyone was paired with somebody except me. I rattled around in my massive double king suite overlooking the magnificent Papagayo Bay, fiddling with the air-conditioning and lights and trying to decide which bed was more desirable. My arrival at the reception threw a pickle in the cheesecake when I asked to pull up a chair at one of the tables of six—a seventh would mar the symmetry of the entire room and the natural order of the table itself. I eventually was seated with a group of young, single adolescents at the overflow table, though the display of fondling suggested that if they were not paired up on arrival, they would be by dessert. After some adolescent chit-chat, I fled to my room to read the room service menu (traveling light means not carrying a book) but not before popping my head into the disco, where couples were butt-cheek to butt-cheek, dancing to the romantic rap of Elvis Crespo. I vowed never to go to a wedding alone again, at least not in the land of *amor.*

I forage for more information on the cheapest burrows—that is, less than $15 a night. The tour guide looks at me as if I am asking him to locate the town's underground septic tanks on my map. I thank him anyway and return to my seat. Below the belly of the plane is the infamous Bay of Pigs, where Cuban exiles unsuccessfully attacked their native soil during the John F. Kennedy administration in 1962.

On landing, the guide clearly takes pity on me, offering me a ride to the resort in his waiting tour bus even though it's a mere 2 kilometers away. As we zoom over the bridge, we pass oil factories chain smoking some obnoxious weed and little houses cowering in the haze. A little farther and the scenery suddenly changes—the road wends around a lakeshore dotted with hotels, bars, and dollar shops lit white and bright like a dental surgery. The bus stops at different hotels to disgorge its occupants and their nice luggage and Nikon lenses. Eventually, the driver looks back and asks where I am going. I point to a piece of pavement in front of a hotel and ask to be let off there.

As soon as my bike and bags hit the ground, some minders from the hotel step forward to determine if I am ready to check in. I unfold the bike, which causes quite a stir, and ask about cheap places to stay. When they understand that I am not going to leave black tire tracks across their pink travertine lobby, they switch into Cuban mode and give me addresses of a couple of nearby *casas* where I might be able to stay for $20 to $25 a night. The only other option is a hotel starting at $36 a night.

I often wonder what these Cubans, who earn less than $10 a month, think of someone blowing more than three times that amount on just one night's "shower, shit, 'n' shave." Varadero is among the few places where there are officially no licensed *casas*. The idea being that you stay in a designated tourist hotel, enjoy three to ten days of bridled sun and fun, and then go home, leaving your dollars on the nightstand, *gracias y adiós.* My Lonely Planet guide says that for one in three foreigners, usually planeloads of Canadians and Europeans, Varadero is their only experience of Cuba. And that's just the way Fidel likes it.

By now it is dark and the tourists are snug indoors, bathing themselves under hot showers and blotting themselves with fluffy towels before heading out to the nearest all-inclusive watering hole. As I pedal slowly along a dimly lighted street, shadows morph into people who ask if I want a room for the night. Given my information that the average private room rate here is around $25, I bump up my strict $5 to $10 budget to $15. There are many shaking heads until one lad agrees to the price and leads me through some back streets to a house.

I am surprised and pleased to discover that ordinary Cuban neighborhoods coexist in the crevices between the glitzy Varadero hotels and restaurants. Little concrete and timber cubes huddle beneath the giant concrete and glass cubes, shacky eateries back onto air-conditioned pizza parlors, and weed lots flank manicured grounds with artificial ponds. Naturally, the town sports one of the ubiquitous Coppelia ice creameries, the Varadero incarnation looking like a grotesque concrete Legoland.

I am taken to the secluded side entrance of a house and received by a twenty-something named Ariel. There is some quiet talk between him and my tout. Ariel tells me that he will have to give $5 of the $15 to the tout, so for $10 my stay is not really worth it to him.

I ask, "Isn't $10 for one night better than nothing for the same night?"

He shows me to the room.

Of course my cheap deal comes at a price. That night I accept his invitation to accompany him on a stroll through town and along the beach. We haven't walked far when he makes a lunge at me and repeatedly tries to kiss me. I had been forewarned about the Cuban male ("Beware of Don Juans"), but this is my first paws-on encroachment. Undeterred by my less-than-romantic response, he then asks me to sleep with him that night. Fortunately, my room has a lock. A double one.

* * * *

I sleep fitfully, flashing back to those long hours with the world's worst sailor. I get up in the morning and wash the salt out of everything. Despite having put all my stuff in plastic bags, everything is wet, even my carefully sealed packet of matches. Ariel appears at breakfast, friendly and chatty but noticeably distant, perhaps due to my ego-squelching rejection. His mother fries my two bread rolls in fat, and I eat them with sticky, sweet *guayaba* paste and juice purchased from the dollar shop over the road. I chat with her cousin, Marta, who has dropped by. Yet again, the conversation turns to the scarcity of food, money, and clothes. I ask why, despite this scarcity, hardly anyone I have met so far grows their own vegetables or raises their own livestock or even keeps a couple of hens in the backyard for eggs.

"Cubans are lazy," Marta says.

She goes on to assert that Fidel has conditioned his people to accept a handout and that, meager as it is, it quells the hunger to take the initiative.

"Everyone complains," she says, "but no one does anything about it other than to continue to complain about too much work and too little food."

Using my own rudimentary theorizing, I reason that perhaps Castro, one of the cleverest heads in the dictatorship business, sees clearly how other poor nations generate income using brawn and brain in varying proportions of each. Tourism, which requires almost 100 percent brain and no backhoeing, is the quickest, cleanest, and most profitable industry of all. A planeload of Canadians, Germans, or Italians arrives twice a day; the passengers dump their dollars on the side table and leave almost as quietly as they came, ensuring minimal danger of contaminating the local waters with outerworldly bacterium— news and views and loose-fit Levis.

In this way Castro shows his people how easy it is to extract ten times their monthly wage from a foreigner just by giving him a pillow, a sheet, and a minibar, and how if you be nice to that paleface and give him directions to the nearest *paladar* . . . who knows? Even the children are picking up on it. *"Regálame un dolar?* Geef me a dollar?" they chime as easily as asking for the time.

It works, because fortunately for them, most of Dollarworld has pity and compassion for this nation. I hear stories of tourist buses driving to the town of Trinidad spewing ballpoint pens, coins, and sweets from their tinted windows and watching the kids grovel. Yes, why toil and sweat for that extra tomato or cup of rice? Just use your Cuban brain.

"Brain over brawn" has given Cuba an international reputation for excellence in medical research, even though its best doctors earn only around $25 a month. Many people come to Cuba for bargain-basement surgery and therapy that cannot be done elsewhere at anywhere close to the price.

Thus, Castro is developing a nation of resourceful and intelligent people who excel in their fields, be it hustling or heart surgery. But if there is a stress point in the structure, it is where an individual reaches for the stars but hits his or her head on the low ceiling of communism.

"The natural thing is for people to want to strive and be rewarded accordingly," says Marta, "but no matter how well you do, your salary stays the same. Everyone is equal. But equality doesn't raise your standard of living. So everyone wants change." It is neither the first nor the last time I hear this viewpoint.

• • • •

I jump on the bike and head toward the end of the Varadero Peninsula, some 20 flat kilometers along a straight, mostly empty highway. Yes, this is Miami Beach with a few more palm trees and a bit of poverty thrown in for local color. According to the map there is a vast natural reserve at the tip of the promontory, including a place to camp. I stop for a 75-cent pizza, three times the price of a pizza elsewhere. The service is slow and off-hand with a touch of attitude, the disease of the dollar.

As I head farther north on the still-empty highway, the landscape changes from clusters of local houses hiding between medium-rise hotels to sweeping, stand-alone resorts perched on a manicured ridge. Unfortunately, a front has arrived, creating a hurricanelike headwind such that I am pedaling at a near standstill. With some difficulty I turn into the Meliá Las Américas Resort, which Lonely Planet not only describes as a "shrine of contemporary mass tourism" but also recommends a stroll around.

It is cocktail hour, and I am prepared. I push my bicycle up the marbled ramp. The bellboy, dressed like the big bass drum player in a Salvation Army parade, wheels my bike to a storeroom and parks it amongst the fancy luggage.

From my bicycle bag I take my packable little black dress.

This remarkable piece of equipment folds into the size of a pair of socks, dries in an instant, and with a simple change of footwear quadruples as a nightdress, beach dress, long skirt, and drop-dead evening dress. Adding a tight black T-shirt dresses it down. Remove the T-shirt, and one is ready for a martini and Mr. Right Now. For a moment I flirt with the idea of spending the night here, but at $170 a single, the fantasy swiftly passes. Families and couples traipse about, faces fixed with that vaguely fish-out-of-water expression packed especially for their once-a-year resort blowout, a firm determination to enjoy the $5.00 orange juice and the organized aerobics hour.

I slide into the bar and make like a resident. After a few

minutes I feel like a carp in a car dealership and slide out again. Next door to the hotel is the DuPont mansion, a stuffy Eurocentric shrine to tycoonism. The guidebook says something about half-price drinks in the top-floor bar at happy hour. Being a typical opportunistic cyclist, I go up to investigate this claim. As usual, my book is out of date.

By this time I have had my fill of seeing how the other half holidays. I return to my bike to do a quick costume change and head back to my $15 digs at the unfashionable end of the peninsula. The headwind is now a roaring tailwind that picks me up and blows me away from this tabernacle of tourism that is somewhere, yet somehow nowhere, in Cuba.

8

LA CASA DE LOLITA

After two days of battling the constant wind in Varadero, I've had enough. The cold front has blown everything off the beach except for a couple of diehard wind worshippers. It is still blowing a gale as I wheel my bike out of the secret entrance to Ariel's house. His mother stops me and whispers that, next time, I can stay for $10 a night, but . . . *shhhhhhhh*.

My plan is to pedal east along the coast as far as possible, then loop back through the central-western towns of Santa Clara, Sancti Spíritus, Cienfuegos, and Trinidad and finally return to Havana.

It is not long before I discover that the wind that stymied the boat ride to Trinidad is the same on the north coast of Cuba as well. It's a capricious and gusty side wind that on several occasions attempts to scoop up my packhorse and hurl it and me against passing trucks. I hang on for dear life, but after an hour I get only as far as the cemetery of Cárdenas, an unfashionable town 15 kilometers down the road.

I reevaluate my route. The last time I encountered this problem was on the far north coast of Scotland, between

Bettyhill and Thurso. After several near-flings into passing oil tankers, I decide to take refuge in a bus shelter and debate my options over a banana sandwich. A truck came by and offered me a ride, hoisting my bike on top with his pallet lifter. Thus, I was spared a potentially dangerous section of the trip. Some hardcore cyclists might sneer at my lack of resolve, but I figure that at the end of my life, it's not going to make much difference how I got from Bettyhill to Thurso, only that I did.

So, yes, I could get a ride. Or I could return to Matanzas, about 50 kilometers back in the direction from whence I came. I could then take a train to the far eastern end of the country, known as Oriente, and work my way back toward Havana from there. Given that the prevailing winds are coming from the northeast, it seems like a logical plan.

Midday I hitch a ride back to Varadero on a passing lorry. The driver happily accepts a dollar for that short distance. During this ride I lose my water bottle, with its curvaceous, neoprene zippered cover, which bounces out of its cage and away. Although riding in this new direction is now a breeze, I take a second truck ride to speed things along. The second driver suggests that he leave me on the *autopista,* the main highway that runs through the center of the country, where I can get a ride for a couple of dollars instead of the $30 train fare. He also warns me that although truck drivers are generally noble and upstanding citizens, the odd one may ask me for a bit of a cavort in the coolroom in lieu of a dollar. I *ummm* and *ahhhh* and decide to take the train to avoid any coolroom conundrums.

The driver goes out of his way to deliver me to the Matanzas railway station and refuses any kind of payment. "I have money," he says simply, showing me a fat wad of 20-peso notes.

The station is a concrete room with several people in chairs waiting to board the 6:00 P.M. twelve-hour overnight train to Santiago de Cuba. The fare is 27 pesos, which is $1.35 if you are a Cuban or $27 if you are a foreigner. The station staff ask me for my passport and tell me that the bike will require a special carriage. They assure me that the scheduled train has one. Next, they insist that I move my bike and bags to an official holding bay in an adjacent building.

At this point a Chinese Cuban and his small daughter, who have been watching with interest, step forward and offer to carry my bags to the holding bay. They live in Santiago, and after telling them my plans I notice that they do not extend an invitation for me to visit. I am mildly surprised, so accustomed am I by now to the Cuban *"mi casa, tu casa."* Santiago must be a big city. I buy them a soft drink, which they gratefully accept.

At the holding bay I am charged a dollar for each item, making it $4.00 in all. Of course the rate for the Cuban next to me is one-twentieth of that. As far as I can tell, the staff merely watch my stuff sitting in a pile behind the counter until the train arrives, then carry it across the tracks and load it on, something I can do myself with the numerous offers of help I receive from bored or inquisitive patrons. The official behind the counter is so insistent about these charges that I pay, but not without a protest to kill some time.

••••

The train arrives and there is a rush to climb aboard. And then the realization: This train does not have the promised "special carriage." The uniformed lackeys manning the train shake their heads. No way can I put the bike on the train; I will have to leave it behind. I tell them that this is impossible, and with less than three minutes to convince them otherwise, I become desperately theatrical and show them how the bike can fold into half the size. Then I push the package onto the train before they can successfully protest. They are so dumbfounded by my act of Houdinism that they stand there for a perplexed second, mouths open, dying to deny me passage; then the train starts to roll and I am on my way. It is truly a close call, and I can only thank the foldability of my Bike Friday for getting me out of the jam.

Once on the train, I discover that my designated seat is some seven carriages farther back from where my bike is now wedged. As if reading my mind, a blue-uniformed guard approaches me and requests an extra $5.00 to *guardar* my bike and belongings, although it soon becomes apparent that I will be the one doing most of the guarding. Thus I have been fleeced for $9.00 total since arriving at the station.

I wedge everything I can in the corner of the train, hiding anything remotely tempting, which is really the whole damn package, and reluctantly leave the guard with his windfall to find my seat. The train is an old, dingy cattle cart with cracked vinyl seats and a faint odor of piss that gets worse as I pick my way through the carriages. The normally sunny Cubans filling the seats seem hollow-eyed and pallid, melting into the dusty torn-up floor and yellowed walls and the stench of toilets washed without disinfectant.

Despite the unappetizing ambience, I suddenly get a lightning attack of hunger pangs. The refreshment carriage offers chocolate, juice, and *el plato del día* (dish of the day), a small cardboard box filled with rice and lentils, pig liver, and a tough bun, all stone cold, for 6 pesos. I am famished to the point that I buy one while the Cubans look on, shake their heads, and say I am *valiente*; they wouldn't touch it. I leave most of it uneaten and chalk it up to another taste experience worth stopping once for.

• • • •

I pick my way back to my seat. My neighbors are a group of Argentinean backpackers; a young German called Michael who wants to climb Pico Turquino, Cuba's highest mountain; and a Danish girl called Lena who has been traveling in Latin America for some time.

Everything seems to be going smoothly. Then suddenly, *BANG*.

It resonates throughout the carriage. The train shudders to a halt. Lights flicker to black. A faint smell of petrol wafts down the aisle. Michael, clearly a former boy scout, leaps over his seatmate and goes out to investigate with both his halogen headlamp and flashlight drawn. He returns with the grim verdict: The train has squashed a petrol tanker that had somehow wandered across the tracks. The full tank has been flung seven carriages backward; in fact, I can make out its crumpled form through the window in the darkness. There is talk of two victims, the tanker driver and the woman in the passenger seat.

"You don't want to go down there," Michael says. "The cabin of the tanker is wrapped around the nose of the train like tinfoil."

We sit waiting, waiting, waiting. About an hour after the collision, we suddenly hear a terrible wailing in the darkness outside.

The talk on the train is that it is the tanker driver's wife, who has turned up at the scene of the accident. The dead female passenger was her husband's secret lover. How my fellow passengers deduce this I know not, save asking the woman herself or extrapolating from the last episode of *la novela*.

The poor woman eventually stops wailing. We wait some more, and it is growing cold, very cold. I make the epic eight-carriage journey back to my bike to drag out the few items of warm clothing I packed, thinking Cuba was a hot place. Then the Argentinean backpackers light up cigarettes. I nearly jump out of my seat to throttle them, given the proximity of the gas tank and the lingering odor of petrol. But it is one of those occasions where in tiredness and apathy you just sit there and fume, much like in a cinema when someone answers a mobile phone.

Eventually the train starts rolling again. I sleep a little. We are still rolling at daybreak. Still rolling at lunch. We reach Santiago de Cuba at 3:30 P.M., nine hours after our estimated time of arrival.

While on the train I chat with José, a Cuban who has a *casa particular* for rent. When I tell him my budget, he suggests that I stay instead with his ex-wife, Lolita, who lives a few doors down from his house and does not have a license. The deal is $10 a night, including a simple nonmeat breakfast and dinner. He tells me that she earns very little as a cleaner and secretary in a hospital and that my contributions will help her a great deal. Michael is also game to stay with Lolita. However, when we get off the train, a couple of hustlers accost the throng of backpackers and offer accommodations—including a bed, breakfast, lunch, and dinner—for $5.00 a person. Even I think this offer is too cheap. Both the infernal Argentinean faction and the guidebook-brandishing Canadian hippie faction try to screw José down even further, arguing that there are many *casas* to choose from.

I can see Michael hesitate, seduced by the apparent cheap price and the attraction of hanging out with a group. José says that he can do a flat rate of $13 on the same three-meals basis, a bargain in anyone's language. The Argentineans counter with $12.50, but José shakes his head. Both factions then turn to the hustlers, and José is out of the running. Michael, a young twenty-something, decides to stick with the young twenty-something group. Somewhat allergic to groups, I stay with José, who is already walking away, shaking his head.

"I do not like the sound of this conversation," he says. "I would rather not have the money than have this kind of people in my house."

We walk through the narrow cobbled streets of Santiago de Cuba, a tightly built, colonial city of thin houses with tiny staircases of three steps going up to the door. Lolita will be home at 5:00 P.M., so José leaves me to wait in the house opposite hers. The house is a licensed *casa particular,* and inside I hear the voice of Lena, the Danish backpacker I met on the train. The *señora* is all smiles and graciousness and offers me coffee and food. She affects a manner I have come to recognize in many others with licensed *casas* and those without: This is a business.

At 5:00 on the dot Lolita arrives, a fleshy black woman with soft eyes and a smile to match. Her house is a tiny, crumbling time capsule wedged in a crevice of colonial Santiago de Cuba. After my ordeal on the train, I decide that this is a place to stop running and to rest for longer than a few hours, perhaps even for days.

• • • •

Each morning at Lolita's house I wake and open the two little shutters in the front doors to let in the mournful cries of *"tomates . . . cebolla . . . ajo . . ."* (tomatoes . . . onion . . . garlic . . .) and the clack-clacking of wheelbarrows trundling through the narrow cobbled laneway.

Lolita goes to work every morning at 7:30 sharp, to a hospital job that pays her $5.00 a month. With this pitiful salary she buys food, cleaning products, or an item of clothing—just one of the above. On the table she leaves me a small plate of scrambled eggs, two bread rolls toasted with a scrap of cooking oil, and a jug of freshly squeezed orange juice. I am aware that she's given me her daily ration of one bread roll plus that of her estranged husband. On the faded walls are photos of her wedding day, in which her ex is blocked out by happier photos of herself, pregnant before her miscarriage. He left her while working in another part of the country, and she attributes the loss of her baby to her heartbreak. Such things are accepted with a sigh in Cuba, the paradox being the intense closeness of family married to the accepted waywardness of the Cuban male. There is even a name for this type of *hombre: picaflor,* or "he who picks [women] like flowers."

I ask José directly about this. He just shrugs.

"It's the Cuban male," he says. *"Mucho calor,"* which translates, very loosely, to "a lotta hotta testosterone."

In the tiny nook of a kitchen, I light Lolita's rusty petroleum camping stove to heat water for a wash and wait for the oily black smoke to disappear. Outside, water comes trickling from a pipe every five days. It is collected in three large drums, the reserve for the coming dry week. I stand in the waterless concrete shower, ladling cupfuls of hot water over my head, and let the spillage fall back into a bucket so as not to waste a drop. I am careful not to use Lolita's small bar of soap though she freely offers it, for it must last her a month. By government decree, toilet paper is found only in the dollar shops, so there is a neat stack of newspaper squares sitting in the dry basin.

"*Leer el culo,*" chuckles Lolita. It translates as a favorite Cuban joke: "Let your asshole read it."

While Lolita is at work, I poke my head through the curtains to her bedroom. I am humbled to see a narrow, squeaky stretcher on a sunken floor where the once-elegant colonial tiles have broken and lifted to reveal the gaping hole below. In my room the dressing table is adorned with empty plastic shampoo and lotion containers left behind by passing guests.

"Decorations," Lolita says when I ask her why she bothers to keep them.

On the wall is a collage of perfume and cigarette advertisements, carefully cut out and pasted onto a square of cardboard. These products are nowhere to be found in the austere, often empty shops where lines of Cubans press their noses against the windows with dollar bills clutched in their palms, waiting patiently to be let into Dollarland.

Each night I eat the most delicious vegetarian food I've tasted in a long time. The fare itself is simple: pumpkin puree, rice, beans, braised cabbage, fried green banana, and maybe a little milk curd for dessert. Yet the flavors are rich and wonderful, full of love and the leaves of thyme that grow in a tin can hanging on the fence.

A small black-and-white television fills the house with drama and hope. Between 9:00 and 10:00 P.M. all of Cuba stops, dries its hands on a towel, and sits down to view *la novela*. There are always three or four hyper-real *novelas* running on the one channel.

• • • •

Lolita makes many apologies for the impoverished state of her house, but somehow this little space is filled with love and light. Most of all, the house is filled with Lolita, a warm and smiling woman who soldiers on in the face of penury and practices her near-fluent German every night, a skill she learned years ago when Fidel sent his people to Russia, Bulgaria, and Germany to assist Cuba's communist brothers. As she practices she dreams of work in Cuba's exploding tourist industry—work that some-day might give her the freedom to buy both food and one of those large bottles of shampoo in the same month.

9

THE SANTIAGO HUSTLE

Lolita returns from work at 5:00 P.M. as usual, flustered from standing in the hot sun for two hours during a televised rally for Elián, the Cuban schoolboy who fled toward Florida with his mother on a rubber raft. Lolita tells me that she and her coworkers were instructed to partake in the rally or lose a month's pay. In a land where a T-shirt can cost a month's wages, only those in the front row at the event were lucky enough to receive the ubiquitous SALVEMOS A ELIÁN T-shirts.

José takes Lena and me to Casa de la Trova, a live music venue found in many Cuban cities and designed primarily for tourists. There are two rooms, one for Cubans and one for foreigners. To hear a duo duel on their guitars in the foreigner bar, the charge is $1.00 per drink. We sit conspicuously amongst other palefaces in their fancy windproof, waterproof wicking travel gear, but the music stops after one more song and the musicians straggle off to the other room.

As we step back onto the street, a young guy latches onto us, or rather onto Lena, desirable with her deep tan and buttery hair. Chatty and disarming, he leads the three of us to a hole-in-the-wall at Calle Heredia #262, where we have the best 5-peso Cuban pizza I have eaten to date: a crispy base topped with what was probably just soy protein but tasted good anyway. José is perturbed by this intruder to our threesome but politely follows along anyway in silence. Of course the young lad expects us to buy him a pizza for his trouble.

We eat our snack on the step opposite the vendor's hole-in-the-wall, then wander down the street. No more than three minutes later, Lena suddenly realizes that she's forgotten her bag, which contains her passport, $4.00 in Cuban pesos, and some prized mementos, including a book and a letter.

The bag has disappeared from the step faster than a Cuban with a ferry ticket to Miami.

With unabashed gal power, enhanced by a $5.00 bill, Lena persuades the street seller who works opposite the pizza shop to take a motorcycle taxi to where he says the chatty and disarming boy lives, for a sniff around. He returns a couple of hours later with concrete evidence: On the kitchen table of the boy's house, he saw a foreigner-type wallet matching the description Lena gave him.

Lena immediately jumps on the motorbike with the informant and heads for the house, but apparently the boy and the wallet have gone into hiding. The neighborhood he lives in resembles a scrap metal dealer's yard, reports Lena later. The family dwelling is little more than four sheets of corrugated iron stacked together like a house of cards. Inside, the boy's mother, a drunk, denies all knowledge of her son's felony.

Lena begs that all she wants is the passport and mementos and that the boy can keep the money, which, to judge from the neighborhood, is perhaps two months' food budget for this family. The woman babbles incoherently. Lena leaves the house empty-handed and faces a decision. To call the police might mean twenty-five years in jail for the boy—the standard penalty for robbing a foreigner. She does not want to be instrumental in that cruel an outcome.

"Call the police," insist the Cubans gathered around the pizza shop. "To let him go will leave him to offend more boldly the next time."

Such stiff penalties exist, they say, to protect Cuba's fattening cash cow: tourism. After much deliberation Lena decides to drop it. The police furnish her with a paper explaining her incident to immigration so that she can move around.

Life in Santiago goes back to sitting on the step.

• • • •

I decide to take it easy and spend a few more days in the character-rich ambience of this colonial city, to refuel and relax in the welcoming presence of Lolita. She warns me about Santiago's infamously tenacious hustlers. Apparently the town is turning out such a high caliber of graduates in this profession that armed police are now a fixture on every corner.

I stroll down to visit the bullet-riddled Moncada Barracks, a solid-looking edifice where, in 1953, more than one hundred revolutionaries led by Fidel Castro attacked Batista's troops stationed in the building. The failed attempt resulted in the cruel torture and murder of fifty-five of Fidel's men. The blurb for the barracks advertises wall-size murals of these gruesome moments for sufferers of excess happiness. The barracks have since been turned into a primary school and museum, and I find it a little disturbing to receive piping commentary from a small, uniformed schoolgirl about this and other bloody memorabilia.

On a street corner I spot a boy selling slices of soft, white cheese in between Cuban bread rolls for 3 pesos each. He is doing a roaring trade with this simple yet delicious snack. I cross the busy road, eating one roll from each hand, and by the time I reach the other side, I cross back to buy a couple more. While I wait in line, a boy about the same age as Lena's robber approaches me in a friendly manner, asking where I am from. My automatic reaction is to snap at him and tell him not to talk to me. Although I immediately feel bad about this projection from Lena's experience, my jaw is now set against Cuban males, and I no longer wait to give them the benefit of the doubt.

More walking leads me to the Hotel Santiago de Cuba, the postmodern pride of the town. An elevator ride to the top floor affords a wraparound view of the city and surrounding mountains. I gaze out toward the dark and rocky coastline that unwinds to the west, the direction in which I hope to be pedaling in a couple of days.

On my way back into the city, I stop at the local Coppelia to eat a 1-peso ice-cream ball and sit in yet another of its distinctively weird concrete gardens. Staff scurry about, dispensing metal trays with one, two, and three scoops in the one and only flavor of the day: melon. The ice cream is a watery sphere of white slush that even the Cubans admit is *más o menos,* or "so-so."

I wander up a narrow street, drawn by the sounds of drumming. The pounding leads me to a museum where a dance troupe is practicing for an evening performance. The males, bare-chested and loinclothed, spin around with females dressed in full skirts and frilly blouses that seem more Alpine than Cuban. The drumming faction belts out Afro-Caribbean rhythms as the dancers whirl around the courtyard. During a break the male dancers approach me to fire the universal Latino male questions on a first meeting: *¿De dónde eres tú?* Where are you from? *¿Casada?* Are you married? *¿Por qué no?* Why not? *¿Tienes hijos?* Do you have children? *¿Por qué no?* Why not? And so on.

Two of the *muchachos* have an excellent grasp of English: Vladimir, a *negro* (an affectionate nickname for a black-skinned man) who wears cool orange shades and a black T-shirt with a glittery motif, and Carlos, a *moreno* (an affectionate nickname for a coffee-colored male) in a white shirt, clean jeans without holes, and a fancy belt buckle. The threads on these boys should forewarn me about their hustling expertise. They're pros.

I ask them where I can buy a good *mojito,* a refreshing Cuban drink consisting of rum, soda, lemon juice, sugar, and mint. They tell me to meet them in the square at 7:00 P.M. and they will take me to a local place that serves *mojitos* and good, cheap food as well. Thinking about the meal Lolita will prepare for me, I tell them that I will eat beforehand, and I suggest that they do the same in their houses. I make it clear that I will not be buying them dinner but simply a *mojito* each.

They look aghast and tell me they did not expect me to buy them anything. They add that "Some Cubanos do this, but this does not show respect."

Pro to pro. Understood.

We leave the performing arts museum together and on the way home stop at a dollar ice creamery that they assure me is superior to Coppelia. The line at the front parts like the Red Sea when I approach with the holy dollar. I am let in ahead of the queue, which makes me feel distinctly uncomfortable. I buy my companions a $1.00 tub of ice cream that is indeed a notch up from Coppelia but no Häagen-Dazs. We pass by the hole-in-the-wall with the kick-ass pizzas, and I buy them one each. They're already scoring well, and I am not even aware of it.

I return to Lolita's digs, where Lena is waiting for me. She's hooked up with some Danish backpackers, so we all agree to rendezvous with my newfound friends at 7:00 P.M. in the park. Now, having traveled solo for so long, I predict that this will lead to a tedious group situation, but having starved myself of conversation in my mother tongue for a month, it seems like a jolly idea at the moment. Lolita has prepared one of her deliciously simple vegetable meals, and Lena decides to share in that instead of returning to her licensed *casa* across the road and eating the officially sanctioned $8.00 meal there. She gives Lena $3.00; I am sure it will be put to good and immediate use.

We arrive at the park at 7:30 P.M., thinking that maybe the boys have left. Of course they haven't.

"Don't worry," Lolita had said as we scurried out the door. "When Cubans say they will be there, they mean it."

* * * *

We have managed to amass a group of twelve travelers, including six from Denmark, two from Holland, and two from Canada.

Vladimir and Carlos are clearly adept at working a group of *extranjeros* (foreigners). They marshal us all toward a barnlike eating and drinking place that resembles a pretty average beer hall, complete with tired-looking staff, hard chairs, and bad acoustics. Despite their earlier assurances, there are no *mojitos* here, just weak beer and juice that comes in tiny, single-suck boxes. Our Cuban chaperones sit down at the head of the table, and everyone orders drinks. On the way to the restaurant, we somehow picked up two scantily clad *muchachas,* obviously friends of Vladimir and Carlos and possessed of the same PR skills, particularly with the stiff and geeky Danish pair, who are lapping it up as if they've never been within sniffing distance of a woman exposing more than ankles and wrists.

Two plates of fried chicken and chips land on the table in front of Vladimir and Carlos. They summon me to their end of the table and insist that I share the chicken with them. I tell them that I have already eaten and return to my intense conversation with the Dutch molecular biologist about strategies for discombobulating the replication of malaria, the topic of his PhD thesis. While I am embroiled in this oddly flirtatious small talk, which is clearly getting the pointy-headed boffin hot, Vladimir interrupts and utters two words in perfectly polite English:

"Money, please."

In suddenly impeccable *español,* I question him about our agreement. Conveniently, he feigns ignorance of his mother tongue. I look at the bill. The damage is slight, around $6.00, but I feel insulted. It is not the money; it is the principle. Principle?

A large part of me shouts, "Principle has no place here! Principle is a luxury only the haves can afford." But word of the disagreement buzzes around the table, and somewhat unnecessarily, all foreigners go into RED ALERT! mode, too polite to dump our chaperones, yet now eyeing their every move like coast guards watching a Cuban wearing floaties on La Altura beach.

Later, with perspective, I am able to understand how an affluent culture can afford to get uppity about the notions of honesty, integrity, and plain old not taking advantage of other people. We call it basic human decency. In a land where people are materially impoverished, it's more like if you've got it to give, you've got to give it.

Vladimir, completely unflummoxed by the chain of events as if it is all in a day's hustling, breezily announces that he is escorting the group to a disco where the entrance fee will be $2.50 a person, which includes a drink. The two *chicas* giggle, their bangled arms now encircling the necks of the two Canadians. The Danes are vocal about the idea, complaining loudly that they certainly will not pay for these four opportunists and not giving a damn that the Cubans probably understand every word. Lena, significantly soused on the empty bottle of rum lying on the table, ting-tings a glass with a spoon to get attention, then proceeds to deliver an eloquent soliloquy about how we are enjoying ourselves as guests in this country, thanks to our hosts, and how sad it would be to ruin the camaraderie . . .

"Why not show our newfound friends what we are made of?" she implores. "If we divide the four entrance fees amongst the twelve of us, it will be barely a dollar each."

No one particularly wants to be singled out as Mean Mr. Mustard, so like a derailed train, the group lurches out of the bar and into the street, swept along in the skippety air-soled slipstream of Vladimir, the Pied Piper of Santiago.

However, even his magical powers cannot seduce our motley mob into agreeing unanimously on even one venue. For the next hour the group snakes from club to club, some factions complaining about the music emanating from within, some harping about the presumptuousness of our chaperones, some complaining about the state of world peace in general so that we never physically enter any particular doorway but mill about outside, engaging in loud, multilingual arguments. If I were

Vladimir, I would leave us stranded at the last lamppost. But a foreigner is a passport into one of these clubs, so I can see why his team is so anxious to stick with the program, even though he must wonder exactly what moon this mob fell in from.

I finally give up on the mindless groupthink, say goodnight, and sneak back down the darkened street to my *casa*. On the way I am bailed up by a group of tanked Cubans who want me to come to their house right there and then. One of them, a sinewy black *chico,* insists that he is on the Cuban boxing team training for the Sydney 2000 Olympics. He regales me all the way to Lolita's front steps, whereupon the little porthole in the door slides open and Lolita's face appears, sternly surveying the source of all the 2:00 A.M. chatter.

"*Cuidado*" (be careful), she says once I am safely inside alone. She rubs the back of her hand with a forefinger, this being the Cuban sign for black skin.

She tells that me if anyone gets into trouble in Santiago, it almost always involves someone with black skin. She rolls her eyes when I tell her that I met a Sydney Olympics contender. "*Mentiras*" (lies), she snaps. "They will invite you to their house, and next day, when you get home, all your things and the things in the house will be gone."

I tell her of my night with Vladimir, and she recounts a sad tale of a tourist who went out with a group of Cubans. They ate and drank and the girl went to the bathroom, leaving her bag on the table in confidence. When she returned her *amigos* were gone, leaving a beer-soaked bill where her bag once was.

"You'd be really fucked, wouldn't you?" asks Lena when I relate this story to her the next morning. She seems weary and just a little angry after her cavort on the town.

"Stupid Danish!" she spits over her banana when I ask her

how the night with Vlad the Lad finished up. She says the group continued from venue to venue, splitting off until it was just Lena and the Cubans left doing the lurching.

"They kept complaining about the music and asking to see another option . . . typical, stupid Danish."

. . . .

The day is still young, so I decide to take the bike out for a spin to the seventeenth-century Morro Castle, about 10 kilometers out of town on the coast.

The castle was built to protect Santiago from pirates. The Carretera Turística (Tourist Highway) wends its way along the bay and offers splendid views of desolate factories and smoking chimneys on the far bank. I arrive at Marina Punta Gorda, a place on the water that features a nice bar and pier. From here you can also catch a ferry to Cayo Granma, a fairytale island just inside the bay and sheltered from the Caribbean Sea.

While I sit in the open bar slurping a juice, a nicely painted ferry sidles up to the pier.

"Tourist ferry, $3.00," says the man behind the bar.

I ask for directions to the nontourist ferry, which the guidebook says is 10 centavos, or a tenth of a peso (half a cent). I am pointed down the road to a dirt track from where you can see the tireless platform ferry putt-putting between the three points in its triangular route connecting island to mainland. When it arrives I roll my bicycle onto the plank deck and pay another half a cent for the extra baggage. We stop at the Morro Castle drop-off point and, to my surprise, Lena gets on, having hitched from Santiago.

Cayo Granma is a small conical island that floats like a

scoop of ice cream in a glass of soda between the headlands of Santiago Bay. A cave tunnel runs from one side through to the other. There is a church perched on the top of the island, a cobbled footpath running around its circumference, and quaint rustic houses with flower gardens strung out along the path. We get off and make for the local restaurant on the side of a hill—but not before some charming Cubanos on the boat invite us to an alternative lunch at the family home, where we can have lobster for $10, they say.

At 1,000 percent profit, it's no wonder they are so persistent. In Cuba you receive many invitations to partake in a variety of activities with the general aim, well meaning or otherwise, to share your dollars. Sometimes it is just easier to say no. We extricate ourselves as gracefully as we can and keep walking. We arrive at the restaurant. On the menu is hamburger, roasted chicken, and a sweeping 270-degree view of the bay and the mainland. Lena and I take a table, sip a juice, and look out at the glimmering sheet of blue water stretched between us and the far shore. I think, *This is good.*

This is good.

I often lapse into circular debates with myself (and whatever unlucky bastard happens to be within earshot) over whether it is possible for one ever truly to arrive. Is it possible to reach nirvana and remain there? I fancy that it is indeed possible, but it takes some doing, or rather, not doing, according to meditation books.

I have met many people striving to live their dreams in far-flung places. Many have created idyllic cocoons spun from financial speculation, fortuitous life-partner choices, personal sacrifice—any or all of the above. Yet few seem to radiate the serenity, the quiet that may indicate that you have truly "arrived." Despite the materialistic deprivations, I sense this quiet in the people of Cuba. How can this be, in a land deprived of U.S. dollars and democratic freedoms of choice?

I have thought long and hard about this. What man fears almost as much as a humiliation by karaoke solo at an AA meeting is death. Death by natural causes occurs at the lowest rungs of man's hierarchy of needs: from lack of food, lack of shelter, lack of medical treatment, and so on. In order to delay death, man must work for money to trade for food, shelter, medical insurance, and so forth, and he must forever run society's treadmill in order to satisfy those three fundamental needs. "The average man lives in a state of quiet desperation," as I heard someone drunkenly but aptly misquote Thoreau.

In Cuba these needs are taken care of: food by the ration system, shelter by the fact that almost everyone has inherited a roof over their heads, and wellness by an almost-free medical system that is affordable to even the poorest Cuban. Although Cubans may pine for stuff, they know that it is unlikely they will starve, die of exposure, or perish from lack of medical care. They have the *quiet*.

My friend Joel, who spent six years living at the beach in Costa Rica, believes that for most of us, nirvana is a slippery eel. The best you'll ever get, he hypothesizes, are fleeting moments of quietness amidst the maelstrom: when sitting on top of a mountain, taking in a sunrise; when floating in a calm sea; when wandering in an intense, strange city; when washing up the dishes after a homemade lasagna that came out right, not too soggy, not too dry . . . fleeting moments when you allow yourself to pause and think, *this is good.*

Sitting on the terrace of this waterfront dive, with its plastic checked tablecloth and my plate of *pollo asado* and modest scoop of white rice, the sun shining like it's never seen rain, I think, "This is good." To prolong my day trip in nirvana, I order a second plate of chicken.

••••

A young woman approaches us. She holds out a round plastic object and an instruction sheet. It is a contraceptive-pill dispenser, fully loaded.

"Can you tell me how this works?" she asks in stilted English.

A friend from the States sent her five of these devices. Lena goes through the instructions in her superior Spanish.

The young *muchacha* is tall and slender, with small, pointy breasts poking through an ill-fitting bra and a tight top. She is just twenty years old and ripe for the picking by a wealthy, white fifty-something *gringo* on a package holiday—but more likely by a macho Don Juan who will eventually leave her and her babies for her sister.

"No babies for five months," I reassure the girl in my best Spanish. She smiles and speaks to us in clear, correct English as if reading from a textbook. "I am very happy to show you my country, whose main industries are sugar, coffee, and tourism . . ." We let her practice.

••••

"*Los Cubanos son grandes.*" Cubans are big.

I turn my head away but unfortunately not before the image has registered on my retinas: a flaccid black worm hanging out from the young man's trousers.

He sits nonchalantly, squatting on the ground, white teeth bared. I am locking my bike to a tree at the entrance to Morro Castle, and he has approached, trying to sell me cigars. When that fails he flops out his Montecristo for my approval. I sigh and tell him to go pester the tourists in the rental car down the road.

"They have more money than me," I say.

Now, if you relate any story about flashing to someone from an Anglo-Saxon background, they'll probably snigger and suggest that a well-aimed guffaw, kneecap, or gesture (as if peering through a magnifying glass) would have been an appropriately deflating comeback. I have been flashed a few times before in my solo voyages, and my automatic response is never one of these thigh-slapping retorts, but rather an instant nausea tinged with alarm. Why? Because you never know what kind of crazy you might be dealing with. The Cubans to whom I relate this incident are unanimously horrified.

"Sick!" they hiss and tap their temples. Such an unseemly act would normally land the culprit five or six years in prison. Cigar Boy had gotten lucky because of my largesse.

The incident does not deflate the impact of Morro Castle, however. I had made the day trip with a slightly jaded attitude, having gotten all castled- and stone circled–out in Great Britain. But on crossing the drawbridge, I am newly awed. Morro is a huge, thick-walled monument perched at the edge of the Caribbean Sea, with wonderful views from its turrets of the whole of Santiago's mountain-ringed bay. Several interconnected chambers and terraces make it feel like a big old funhouse where you can dart up and down and play hide-and-seek. From the top I can look north to Cayo Granma, that little scoop of an island bobbing in the bay, the tireless taxi boat cutting its way toward it, then away from it . . . toward it, away from it.

I turn my head to gaze at the Sierra Maestra coast, serpenting its black pebbled way into the west, where I will be heading in a day or so. Yes, it is finally time to leave the hustlers, the flashers, and *la casa de Lolita.*

10

THE SIERRA MAESTRA COAST

My last day in Santiago is spent wandering the streets with Lena, inspecting a few licensed *casas* for "next time," to see what kind of lumpy pillow a few extra pesos might buy. As wonderful as Lolita is, a bone in my body is yearning for comfort, and I long for a hot shower that comes from a hole in the wall rather than a hole in a bucket.

In a narrow street we spot a house with its door open and a flower-filled terrace on the roof. The house contains several rooms, each renting for $10 to $20 a night. A hammock strung lazily across the terrace is inviting. In the living room a svelte Cuban couple is taking a backpacker from Sweden through salsa moves. His concentration is intense. Uncharitable thoughts cross my imperfect mind. Something about the hip and butt of the white western male making a salsa sashay look like a duck waddle. The fluid ease with which the Latinos move seems directly related to their attitude toward life.

On hearing of my plans to pedal along the coast the next day, the couple's son, Titín, offers the address of his Aunt Milagro as a place to stop for a night. She lives a mere 18 kilometers outside Santiago, a conveniently lazy first day before my assault on the long and winding Sierra Maestra coastal road, sections of which, until 1999, were under construction and not passable.

We saunter back to our *casa* and sit on the step, eating sliced green mangos with salt, while Lena talks about plans to meet her new boyfriend from Denmark in Baracoa, at the remote eastern tip of the country. To get there one has two choices: Take the scenic road that twists like a lizard's gizzard through the pointy part of a mountain called the Alto de Cotilla, or zip across from Santiago de Cuba on the overbooked twice-weekly flight.

After reading all the hype about Baracoa in my guidebook and listening to Lena swoon about her impending tryst, I make a mental note to visit it one day with a lover. As we sit mulling over our vapid love lives, a tall *negro* comes by with a guitar. I leap to my feet and ask to borrow it. The instrument is little more than a few slats of split wood with rusty strings stretched across it, but this *hombre* has dreams about recording his songs and becoming famous.

I twang out my limited repertoire; he croons in Spanish, then asks if I will go and buy a new set of strings for him. As the shops are now shut and I will be leaving at the crack of dawn the next morning, this is impossible. Or I make it impossible.

I am uncomfortable with playing fairy godmother to the small dreams of the average Cuban, dreams that could quite easily come true with a wave of my wallet, and I don't know why. I balk at lavishing dollars on these needy people yet feel guilty about my privileged status and return ticket out of Havana in a couple of months' time.

• • • •

It is midmorning—not quite the crack of dawn—as I pack and eat the last of Lolita's little heartwarming breakfasts. I slip out of the house and leave her $3 so that she can finally buy the $24 bed she has been saving for over the past six months. I take one last look at her wedding photos. The white lacy meringue of a dress had cost around $25 and the reception at a local resort another $200—*demasiado* (too much), says José. Almost two years saving for a wedding, not uncommon by world standards. People everywhere have similar dreams and debts, only the scale is different.

• • • •

I pedal out of town following the signs, an easy path to the Sierra Maestra. When hunger pangs strike I stop at the first beach I come to, a little *campismo* with concrete shacks that are now becoming a familiar sight. I find a tree to sit under and eat my breakfast. A young man, hired to watch over the empty *campismo* bunkers, strides over to make sure I am not bringing trouble. He sits beside me. Some kids come over and demand ballpoint pens. Hustling has reached the city fringes and is now crawling open-palmed, slowly but steadily, along the coast.

Newly completed, the road is a spectacular and winding black ribbon flanked by scree-smattered slopes on one side and a pebbled shoreline on the other. I have barely gotten on the bike before I find myself coasting into the village of Boca de Dos Ríos, or Mouth of Two Rivers, where I search for Titín's Aunt Milagro.

It is not difficult since there are just five houses in the entire village. She lives in a cement-and-dirt-floor cubicle beside a gray, pebbly beach with her sixteen-year-old niece Nayra, a quiet girl afflicted with congenital arthritis in her knees. At times Nayra cannot walk, so Milagro rubs a mentholated gel into her kneecaps to try to keep them warm. The ointment is expensive, and the family in Santiago with the roof terrace and guests like the gyrating Swede help her to pay for them. Despite my rule about not eating meat when traveling, Milagro persuades me to eat a delicious piece of *res* (steak) fried in copious quantities of onion and garlic on the blackened grate of her fuel stove. I am disturbed at how carnivorous I suddenly become. I feel like Dracula after Ramadan. The meat is *escondida,* slaughtered in the backyard of someone's house and distributed amongst friends, as opposed to the officially sanctioned and subsidized rations issued from the *bodega.* Milagro piles my plate higher with a second helping.

"*¡Come, come!*" she instructs. "Eat, eat!"

After dinner I help Nayra with her homework. One of her subjects is entitled *Valores,* or Values. The pages of her crumpled exercise book are full of her hesitant, crooked cursive, and as I turn the pages, I read the topic headings: *Honesty. Integrity. Authority.*

The words ring out from the page. As she reads aloud the house is filled with words of somber wisdom and the sea goes quiet. *Honesty. Integrity. Authority.* Mine were "reading, writing, 'rithmetic." I see that something useful was missing from my own early education.

Milagro comes into the room to rub some balm on Nayra's knees. It is a little chilly. I notice that there are only sheets on the beds—no blankets, except for a single holey rug that Nayra spreads over her legs.

"Nobody here has blankets," Milagro says. "They're too expensive."

I pull out the blanket I stole in defiance from an airline that took two days instead of two hours to get me home last year. It is now part of my outdoor survival kit, but it could have so easily enhanced this family's indoor survival kit. Thinking back, I could have, should have, left it for Nayra. Coulda, woulda, shoulda.

As I am preparing for bed, Milagro brings in a kind of nightcap designed to promote sweet dreams. As far as I can tell it is simply a cup of sugar dampened with a little water, and a half a sip of the viscous liquid is all I can swallow. She goes over and tucks Nayra's knees under the blanket and gives her a gentle, loving kiss. I curl up in my bed and close my eyes. My last vision is the darkened silhouette of Nayra huddled under her rug, backed by the sound of boats clonking together in the calm sea.

• • • •

Milagro scribbles down a couple of addresses, including one that simply says, "La China, La Bodega, El Uvero."

I decide that El Uvero, 60 kilometers down the road, is my next stop. I give Milagro $7.00, which she initially refuses. After I tell her that it is for Nayra's knees, she gives me a look of grateful reluctance and takes it. She says she will write to me and tell me what she buys Nayra with it. Nayra is already dreaming. She shows me a pair of tattered plastic sandals with faded glitter embedded in the plastic and a broken strap. My money could buy a new pair of those, and there would be some funds left over. I wave them good-bye, but they do not go back inside until I am gone from view.

The road starts to undulate. The low hills to my left are rising steeply and becoming reminiscent of the foreboding granite cliff faces of western Scotland. ("Try to resist making comparisons; it dilutes the experience," said a friend when I compared the sparsely lit, darkened hills of Lago de Garda in northern Italy with the suburban, streetlit environs of Canberra, Australia's planned national capital, where I spent most of my formative years.)

I stop pedaling at the edge of a bluff to eat the rice and beans that Milagro piled into my lunch box, and I ruminate vaguely on my future as my eyes rest on the pounding sea below. The food is finished before my future is sorted out, so I lid my lunch box and climb back on the bike.

I pass what looks like happy hour at a store embedded in the foothills of the magnificent Sierra Maestra. The mountain rises up behind the store like a giant tree-covered wall, dwarfing the handful of Cubans lolling about to the faint *thud-thud* of taped salsa music. The mountain is perfectly lit by the blazing afternoon sun. I ride past, thinking that I should stop and take a picture, but I keep riding. The picture is fully developed and framed in my mind, and that is where it will stay. I have rolled past many moments with an involuntary 5x3 viewfinder tattooed on my corneas, but lately my camera has become somehow inaccessible, preventing me from canning memories. The more I travel, the more pictures I take without it.

I roll into El Uvero and know that I have arrived someplace special. El Uvero is the site of a major battle fought by Fidel's guerrilla army. The village is neat as a pin despite the dry dirt roads pleading for rain to fall. I stop a woman walking with a large sack and show her my address: La China, La Bodega, El Uvero. She points a finger ahead to the beginning of a dirt path. The path leads to an open shack decked out with shelves: *la bodega*. In its darkened recesses I can make out cauliflower, a couple of cabbages, and some withered carrots. There is no sign of La China.

A little boy appears and offers to take me to La China's house, a little farther along the bumpy path. I allow myself to be led to a cul-de-sac where the occupants of a cluster of small dwellings come out and surround me. I am struck by the riot of flowers spilling over the front porches and fences. La China finally arrives home; she finished work at 5:00 P.M. on the dot. It always strikes me as strange how people in the most remote parts of the world still live by the punctual tick-tock of that infernal invention, the clock.

• • • •

Xiumara, or "La China," as she is affectionately called on account of her semi-slanty eyes and black hair, is a half-Chinese, half-Cuban woman born in Cuba with about the same random probability as I was born in Australia. We both muse about our paths: Her father had come from Communist China to work in Communist Cuba and married a Cuban girl. My father had applied to study in the United Kingdom, Australia, and the United States and ended up in Australia simply because it was the first country to reply. La China, in time, had married a Cuban. I, in time, had shacked up with an Australian. She is still married. I am still dithering.

My Australian passport disallows me from working in any country except my home country. As often as I drat my luck, I meet people in exotic locations who yearn to see Australia and would give their right arm to live and work there. "Man will travel the world to find what he seeks at home." I wonder who wrote that. Maybe I did. I am starting to long for home, wherever that might be. I have a theory that I may never find it, having been born yellow in a white country, straddling two worlds with one foot planted in each, a kind of cultural schizophrenia.

La China shows me a faded photo of her father, which reminds me of my Nanna's old photos of my ancestors, their somber faces looking Mao-ward.

La China's husband, Elizardo, a tall, handsome Cubano, walks in the door. He works boats and often helps out down the river at the tourist hotels. We eat. As I help wash up, I remark to La China that she and Elizardo look happy and content. She shrugs her shoulders and makes a hand motion and says, "At times."

I wander out back and inspect their garden: a couple of banana trees, an avocado tree, a few pigs, and a wonderful coconut tree that curves skyward like a smooth banister on a sweeping staircase. La China sees me gazing at the tree and whistles to the little boy who brought me to her house. His name is Carlos, a neighbor's son. He shins up the tree, and several of the large green nuts soon thud to the ground. I offer him a peso; he looks me steadily in the eye and shakes a tiny finger from side to side.

"It's to buy an ice cream for your sister," I insist.

He takes the coin, then leaves it on the table. I mention this impressive display of integrity to La China, surprised after the pen and coin panhandling I have experienced with children elsewhere in the country.

"Good training," she remarks.

She shows me to my room, cozy with a comfortable bed under a torn mosquito net. I want to hear more about her life, but there is little more for me to see than what I am seeing moment to moment. Cubans live moment to moment; thus the future for them is not such a scary place.

• • • •

I sleep well and rise early to pack and leave. I cannot really understand why I must leave this serene place after just one day. There is little for me to do, other than live. Carlos arrives at the door and offers to take me to the monument in the village dedicated to Fidel's heroic stand in El Uvero. I follow him and his sister up the dusty road to a manicured park with a massive square spire, on which the names of the lost revolutionaries are inscribed in bronze. A row of tall, impossibly straight and smooth palm trees flanks the gravel pathway like colonnades to heaven. I pass a few minutes gazing at the names, thinking about how they once were flesh and blood and blue jeans and furniture and kids and maybe a TV set. Now they are each two strings of letters separated by a compassionate single space.

I wander back to my loaded bike, lost in thought. La China gives me the name of a friend 70 kilometers farther down the road at a beachside resort called Marea del Portillo. I decide that I can make it if I try.

I try, and I make it. Marea del Portillo consists of two tourist hotels on minimally landscaped grounds on a quiet cove. By this time every fiber in my body longs for a hot shower and some non-Cuban food, like a Caesar salad with fresh anchovies and blue cheese dressing. One of the hotels, Farallon del Caribe, had been written up by Stephen Psallidas, whom I happened to surf across one evening on the Internet. "Fifty-five dollars, including a buffet breakfast and dinner, unlimited alcoholic drinks and a trip to a coral cay thrown in! Not bad really!" Stephen enthused on his Web site.

The Farallon del Caribe commands an elevated position on the lower slopes of a hillside and beckons with its ultramodern facade and suspended, free-form swimming pool. When you stand on one of the lower steps leading to the pool, the water seems to meld with the still waters of the secluded cove in the distance. I pedal my way up the concrete drive to the marble reception desk staffed by serious and well-starched Cuban concierges.

"Sixty dollars a night, no discount."

I linger on the steps for a while trying to make up my mind. I can easily afford this night of luxury: I am carrying a ridiculous amount of cash, and I've been spending an average of $12 a day. I have not spent this much money on a hotel room for a very long time—years, in fact. There is also the option of seeking out La China's friend, and another bucket bath, in the village.

I am still sitting on the steps when a group of deadly serious touring cyclists bowls up the drive. They left at 5:00 A.M. and pushed it all the way from Manzanillo, over the hill and far away. They've also booked most of the rooms. A support van carrying their stuff is on the way. I try to remember the last time I rode my bicycle without my life-support system. The cyclists regard my small-wheeled bicycle with a certain bemusement, wondering why anyone would want to work so hard. For the umpteenth time since I bought the bike, I explain how its gear ratios are equivalent to that of big-wheel bikes. But the group is already headed for the showers and bar. I decide to do same.

I am shown to my quarters by the handsomest man I have set eyes upon for a long time.

Roberto, a deeply tanned former cane cutter, now plays host to the planeloads of German, Canadian, and French package tourists who eat, drink, and sun-worship their way though this opulent clearing house for the dollar. He has the face and physique of a Hollywood screen hero with a Latino twist, a

Charlton Heston without the soliloquies, a Kirk Douglas with added *huevos*. Most alluring of all, he seems devoid of the mild conceit that usually comes with such a genetic blessing.

I peel my eyeballs away from his general direction and roll my bike into the capacious room, which dazzles with tiles as white as Roberto's teeth, embossed toilet paper folded over at the corners, and scratchy white towels like sandpaper.

Too thirsty to shower and slip into something more comfortable, I go straight to the bar and down four piña coladas in one hit, the first three barely touching the sides. I then proceed to the buffet, which resembles the Last Supper, a long table groaning with massive breads, cheeses, sides of smoked and cured animal, mountain ranges of salad, fruits, sausages, and desserts trailing off to some vanishing point near where a Cuban band is playing "Guantanamera" and hoping for a stray dollar to float their way. In between refilling my plate four or five times, I hide packets of jam and ketchup in my pockets and make a note to return with my cycling jacket so I can slide a poppy seed baguette into each of the arms. In short order I am the one groaning. I know I must lie down soon or I will explode like an overheated Pop-Tart.

I waddle out poolside to where several sun lounges are lined up in anticipation of the night's organized entertainment. They are already occupied by the white-sneaker brigade. I chat with a couple of forgettable boys from Dresden, playing out their yearly ritual: Buy package trip to Cuba, sit in a sun lounge for a week, sip all-inclusive piña coladas until politely tanked, then return to their land of plenty. Fidel's perfect tourists.

"Lady and jellyman, welcome to Cuba! Do you love Cuba? *All raaahht!* Everybody got bingo card? Tonight you win this bottle of Havana Club Rum! *All raaahht!*"

I suddenly feel the urge to leave the area. The slender Cuban entertainment director with massive gold earrings and fluorescent pink lips prances about and spittles down the microphone whenever she has to translate good Spanish to good-enough English. I struggle to my feet to escape and head off for a moonlit stroll around the garden. In a gazebo I meet Roberto and his supervisor, Nelson, splendiferous in their uniforms, and I try to explain to them why a girl staying in a $60-a-night hotel (three months' pay plus good tips for them) would carry a tent and a stove and be looking for a bucket bath in the next town. Nelson says he can tell the difference between tourists with money and tourists without.

"Rich tourists do not arrive on a bicycle with tent and stove and agonize for two hours if they should pay for a hotel room," he says. He invites me to stay with him and his family in Pilón. I say I will think about it. If Roberto is his neighbor, I'll surely go.

• • • •

I go back to my room. I wash out all my clothing and hang it around the room to dry, so that my luxurious habitation soon resembles a college dorm populated by particularly slovenly girls. I sleep and dream, counting German *Apfelkuchens* leaping over picket fences made from poppy seed baguettes washed away by a flash flood of piña colada mix.

The next day I wake bleary-eyed. I stumble to the buffet to see what else I can conceal in my panniers. The dining room is full of Germans, their pasty flesh now slightly reddened; the vast array of cheeses, bratwursts, and pretzels gives no clue that they are, in fact, on an island far from the Black Forest of Germany.

I pack a few things and go out front to wait for the minibus that will take me and fifty others to that coral island with a barbecue lunch and all water sports thrown in, as decreed by my ticket. The minibus glides up, and I enter its immaculately upholstered interior. The door closes with a precision München thunk, and we hum down the highway. Now and then a sleek tourist minibus swooshes past, and I muse how strange it is to be on the inside of the tinted window and not out there, 2 feet below. I also notice that I do not have a clue where I am going now, a strange sensation that disappears the moment that tinted window slides away and I am bike-borne, head to head with the road, the sun, the wind, and the rain.

We finally stop at the edge of a bay where a boat is waiting. My heart leaps to my throat and threatens to asphyxiate me: I notice that one of the crewmen is, for God's sake, Elizardo, La China's husband in El Uvero, to whom I'd boasted about my no-frills style of traveling and to whom I gave a paltry, ungenerous $5.00 for their generous hospitality. Elizardo who gave me the address of a friend in the same town as the expensive hotel I am staying in, so that I might have somewhere inexpensive to stay.

And now I am about to be exposed and humiliated as a liar, a fraud, a shoestring-crying-poormouth since I have clearly chosen to stay in one of the most expensive hotels in Cuba. Elizardo? Is that you?

So many faces roll past me when I travel, like a moving panorama on fast forward, that they don't get etched firmly in my brain. I remember the embarrassment of not being able to tell the difference between two of the Chinese students at my university even though *I'm* as Chinese as a rickshaw driver to the casual observer.

There is no way I can be sure whether that man sitting in the boat is Elizardo. Perhaps it is, and because I ignore him, he feels slighted and does not ask, "Do you remember me?"

Perhaps it is not Elizardo, since there are many Cubans with black mustaches and black curly hair. There are many, many Chinese with slanty eyes and straight black hair. Unable to resolve it, and embarrassed to high heaven, I stay silent.

I wait forever on the deck of the gently rocking boat, even after having vowed never to land a bunion on any boat again after that nightmare hitch with the world's worst sailor.

Our tour boat sets off at last for the island. On arrival it's as if I've landed on the set of *Gilligan's Island:* perfect sand, trees bent just so for shade, groomed paths to stick to. I find a space on the beach to lay my towel, in between sun lounges perfectly lined up and facing seaward. Kayaks, windsurfers, surf skis—all bob in the water at the disposal of the honored guests. Lunch is a Germanic barbecue feast of honey ham, burgers, German sausages, and salad. I borrow a snorkel and mask and paddle out to the reef, making sure that I am still within yelling distance of the shore. Large purple fans sprout from the seabed, wave with the tide, and are interspersed with darting fish. Not bad at all.

At 2:00 P.M. I jump on the shuttle back to the hotel and prepare to leave. I have taken full advantage of my $60 stray from the path of austerity. As I am coasting down the driveway, a merry band of Swiss cyclists rolls up, having covered in one day the 180-kilometer trip from Santiago de Cuba that took me three days. I speak briefly to them, comparing wheel sizes, pretending to be interested in the average speed and cadence of their day's touring. Then I head for my bucket bath in Pilón.

Christmas in Havana: rice, beans, fried pig, *la novela,* and a packable, quick-drying black dress.

Off to get drinking water in Holguín— 1 cent per drum.

I spent New Year's Eve 1999 at Playa La Altura with this coast guard family, who watched over my tent.

Ah, Manzanillo—the town I visited because it had the same name as that of my estranged beau.

The land of the *mogotes*, strange limestone hills in Viñales, Pinar del Río.

"We believe in the Revolution," says the wall.

On the road to Manzanillo.

"When will you come back to La Loma?" asked the *trovador* who taught me "Guantanamera" on top of the big molehill of Holguín.

House with a great water view on Playa Blanca, Holguín.

Langosta libre at Cayos de San Felipe. They almost made up for the nightmare boat ride to nowhere-near-Trinidad with the world's worst sailor.

The multicultural
face of Cuba in
La Palma.

The ration book:
one bread roll per
person per day.

Colonial houses in Cienfuegos, the
town where I was assaulted.

Brutal architecture of the Russian
Embassy in Havana.

A *ponchero* in Sancti Spíritus took a pedal off his old clunker and sold it to me when mine mysteriously disappeared on a truck ride to Havana.

Every book on Cuba has this shot of Che Guevara.

This fellow is off to buy lettuce. Notice his super-clean jeans. The bike is a Chinese Flying Pigeon, a real asset.

Ivan, Mirella, and their only daughter served up a magnificent local meal in Trinidad, including rice and beans, fried plantains, and a $3.00 fish.

With my Bike Friday.

Heading for Havana at high speed. My left pedal mysteriously spun off and disappeared through a crack in the truck bed, I think.

Yoanka the Olympic cyclist and I met in the tray of the truck to Havana.

Yoanka and me in front of a mural that says "To Sydney for the Glory of the Country."

Zaida and daughter welcomed me into their home in Manzanillo.

11

THE HANDSOMEST MAN IN CUBA

The moment I accepted Milagro's address in Santiago de Cuba, my trip took a radical new turn. What started out as a typical bicycle trip, with the goal of covering a reasonable chunk of Cuba each day, is now a moment-by-moment seizure of opportunities lucky-dipped off the back of other opportunities. It may mean riding merely to the next corner to see what's up.

My next destination, just 12 kilometers down the road, is Pilón. Nelson, the guard at the swank Farallon del Caribe Hotel, has given me his address and an invitation to stay the night with his family.

I have confirmed the sincerity of his offer by asking him in three different ways if it is okay to impose upon him. My ex used to parody the middle-class suburban dinner invitation:

"You must come over sometime . . ." (*but for God's sake don't*).

I received a positive answer three out of three times. Of course, I learned from living in Costa Rica that such pre-confirmation is pointless; it serves only to make the invitee less apprehensive, but when the time actually arrives, you may well find your host out of earshot, out of town, or availing himself of a better offer. I recall an enthusiastic invitation from a friend of a friend to watch a DVD movie on his home cinema. On three separate occasions I called to confirm my imminent arrival, and each time he was respectively out of the country, out of town, or out of sorts.

"Face it: He doesn't like you," offered a colleague helpfully, as direct and as Dutch as they come. Sage advice, so why so hard for me to swallow? My Dutch colleague was also dealing with the expatriate blues. He was a cold-water trout in a tropical pond, gulping alcohol and industrial-strength antidepressants in order to survive in paradise.

Lolita, when I consulted her on the topic of sincerity, said, "When Cubans say yes, they mean it, whether there is a dollar in it for them or not. *Sin interés.*" Without obligation.

Yes, despite the increase of hustling, Cubans seem to be made of more substantial stuff. One could say that if you haven't got much going on in your life, you might as well be hospitable. I may be the only person on the planet who sees Cubans as somehow more fortunate than the rest of us. They are sincere because they have not had their lives filled with the commercialism that has bled the heart out of humanity. I keep hearing about the breakdown of the family in western society from God-bothering and religious types. I still do not bother God, nor do I go to church, yet, belatedly, I am starting to see what they've been getting at.

Twelve kilometers later I pedal into a gas station. A brace of Cuban *chicos* at decidedly loose ends spends half an hour insisting that Nelson lives some 20 kilometers farther down the highway, until a deaf-mute man emerges from a dim recess and leads me to the front gate of Nelson's house. I sincerely want to tip the man, but I don't put my hand in my pocket.

Nelson, as chipper in a polo shirt as his starched alter ego at the five-star hotel, invites me in. I sit in his modest living room, a single space with a kitchenette and four simple chairs arranged in a chatty manner on a shiny clay floor, with a curtain concealing the only other room in the house. A warm wind blows from rough square holes that frame glimpses of the backyard, shower, pit latrine, and a half dozen small pigs congregating around the washing line. Nelson's two little children dart in and around the chairs, and his shy wife maintains a respectful distance. She cooks rice and beans and insists that I eat first, setting me a solitary place at the table. It is the foreigner's throne that I am starting to know so well. It still feels awkward.

While I am explaining the story of my life in bad Spanish, Roberto, the handsome bellboy who had shown me my room at the Farallon del Caribe, finally shows up. Here, in the relaxed environment of Nelson's cozy living room, I see just how handsome this young man really is. He has the cut-glass profile of a classic screen hero, but with smooth, malt-colored skin and soft, chocolaty eyes. At just twenty-four, he's already been married twice though miraculously is without offspring and, even more miraculously, is now single again. Nelson has similarly chalked up three marriages, spawning at least one child from each. Roberto informs me that the Cuban male is prone to "restlessness."

We sit around and make small talk about the same kinds of things I have been small-talking about on my trip so far. There isn't a lot else to talk about, given that most Cubans I meet have and will continue to have a predictable life and job; few have had the freedom to generate an outlandish personal past or dream of an even slightly outlandish future.

When it is time for the delectable Roberto to leave, we wander out to the gate. He walks through it, and I close it behind him. We stand shaking hands through a hole in the wire, and then there is that moment of truth, that eternal pause where both of you teeter on the edge of decision, hearts beating, time tick-tocking, knowing that one of you simply has to keep hanging on to those fingers just a little longer than is politely platonic and the gate will push open. I would follow him to his house, where he lives alone; there would be more small talk, and we would disappear to a place where neither of our mothers is looking, and between odd, mismatched sheets and a lumpy, cold bed and a cracked ceiling we would find fleeting heat, love, and gratitude in each other, until with the morning sun streaming across the floor we would part. . . .

I let go of his hand.

• • • •

Excess Baggage

Love is a bulky item
It keeps popping out of my suitcase
Like a great big woolly sweater
Like a hole in the tube of my toothpaste
And I wish I'd left it with the cat
Where it couldn't cause me pain
'Cos I'm travelin' light, I'm travelin' bright
I'm jumping from train to train
And I see you lying beside me

And you tell me I'm not for you
You say I'm just a passing train
And you're a station I'm passing through
And we share a joke about the way we met
Surfing for love on the Internet
And how we found each other at a border post
And together we walked from coast to coast
And I think I'd stop, dead in my tracks
Throw my ticket away
If you held me close and looked me in the eye
And suggested I extend my stay
Love is a bulky item
I'm paying time and time again
I'm paying for excess baggage
And it's giving me a shoulder pain
And you tell me again in case I didn't hear
That for you I'm not the one
And I go to lift that great big bag
And shit, it weighs a ton
'Cos everything inside is wet wet wet
Wet with a thousand tears
And I try to get my love to dry so I can
Face those traveling fears
Of returning alone with no one home
'Cos nobody met my train
And a great big bag with a warning tag that says
I've been it
I've seen it
But what have I gained?

• • • •

Back in the house Nelson is busy preparing a place for me to sleep. I walk through the curtain leading to the other room and find a double bed with one corner of the sheet neatly turned back for me. Over on the other side of the room, Nelson and his wife, daughter, and baby snuggle together in a narrower bed. No amount of persuading can make them change this arrangement. I crawl into the matrimonial bed and, feeling decidedly unmatrimonial, have trouble getting to sleep. I hear them shuffling about.

"¡Coño!"

"Does that mean *puta?*" I ask rhetorically from my side of the room.

I know that *coño* means more than merely "bitch." It is the most common expletive in Cuba and translates loosely to "cunt." It is uttered under such circumstances as stubbing your toe, spilling your coffee, realizing you are hopelessly late. It is the last word, amidst some giggling, that I hear before drifting off to sleep.

In the morning I wake and prepare yet another of my signature bike-rider breakfasts before four bemused sets of eyes: bread rolls stuffed with bananas. I press a $5.00 note into the hand of Nelson's wife. She tries to press it back into my hand, but I tell her it is *un regalito,* a little gift. She smiles and takes it.

• • • •

My next stop is Niquero, a coastal town preceded by a nice gradual climb over a hump that then plummets all the way to sea level on the other side. The town is not mentioned in any guidebook I have seen, but as soon I enter the tree-lined boulevard at the outskirts, it looks promising. My plan is to stop briefly here, then continue along the peninsula to the southwest tip of the country, to a place called Cabo Cruz. La China in El Uvero has given me the address of friends there, and I single-mindedly point my front tire in that direction.

On a corner stands a tourist hotel, not yet open. The main street is bustling with horses, bicycles, and foot traffic. In the center is an expansive square of cracked bitumen that looks like it has been waiting an eternity for a fountain or a basketball hoop or a parking lot to materialize. At the far side are three 15-centavo pizza carts and a couple of juice-in-a-bag vendors vying for the passing peso.

I toss a mental coin and go for the cart with the necklace-laden *señora,* and I get lucky. The fare eclipses that last "best Cuban pizza" I ate in Santiago. The crust is crisp and light like a good focaccia, with a density that suggests flour of some substance. The sauce tastes of real tomatoes, patiently reduced on a stove with homegrown herbs. The cheese is just right, not too thick or greasy.

I eat another. Then another. I decide to try the competition, but I am disappointed. Now completely queasy with pizza, I wash it down with a bag of juice, not really considering where the water might have come from, and then seek refuge from the heat in an air-conditioned dollar store.

I am standing at the back of the store, contemplating the two choices of vanilla cookie on display, namely square or round, when a plump, well-dressed woman to my right turns and smiles at me.

"*Eres Italiana?*" she asks. Are you Italian?

She chats with the ease of someone who is comfortable with foreigners. Her name is Julia, and she speaks of her wealthy Swiss-Italian *esposo* who jets across the Atlantic to make merengue with his Cuban wife and their eight-year-old daughter every two or three months. She invites me back to her house, where she and her mother, brother, and daughter live in comparative affluence thanks to her *esposo:* Goldstar television set in the living room, brand-new frost-free fridge in the kitchen, an Escada jacket in her wardrobe, and duty-free perfumes, shampoos, soaps, and creams that she displays on her dressing table.

We talk about their lives, the same theme of waiting, waiting . . . waiting for her husband to come, waiting for things to change. This, from a household blessed with more good fortune than the neighbors on either side of the fence. It is clear that a Goldstar television set is no substitute for unfettered capitalistic opportunity, freedom to cast a vote, and a choice of shampoo.

The family shows me a yellowing issue of a magazine commemorating Fidel's historic first landing in their town, when he is supposed to have stepped onto the beach and uttered the words "I have come to liberate Cuba."

A gusty wind has reared up and is rattling the frail windows. Julia and her brother entreat me to stay the night, insisting that the wind will make it difficult and dangerous for me to ride to Cabo Cruz. Something inside me decides to believe this pair of noncyclists, so I let them take me on a walk to look for ingredients for dinner.

First, we visit a government farm selling lettuce out of the ground for 1 peso per head. Then we make our way through decrepit back streets to a secret fish supplier in a very poor neighborhood. Everyone in town seems to know that Julia is married to a rich foreigner, so every purchase begins with a haggle. We emerge from that neighborhood with an enormous *pargo* (snapper) for the equivalent of $3.50, "a bit high," sighs Julia. She refuses to let me pay for the fish.

I sit on the porch in a chair and watch a friend of Julia sort stones out of a dish of rice, just like panning for gold nuggets, but throwing the gold away and keeping the silt. Inside, the aroma of fried fish with onion fills the little house. Julia piles my plate high.

That night Julia brings out a pile of photos of herself and Euro-hubby Christian living life in the fast lane in Italy, Paris, and the Swiss Alps. There she is, outside hotels, in the pool, and draped over a shiny red car. She looks happy and content. Julia is in bed by 10:00 P.M. I climb into my side of her bed and lie in the place where her *esposo* will rest his worldly head not long from now. I drift off, resting my eyes on the dark shock of her hair and breathing in the odd fragrance of French perfume on my pillow.

• • • •

The next morning the family surrounds me as I start loading up the bike. They seem even more intensely interested in me than the night before. One by one they do their best to convince me that Julia's marriage to her *extranjero* (foreigner) is wonderful, that Julia's brother would make a fine husband, and do I not think he is *guapo?*

I glance at this timid, studious boy who does not reek of *picaflor.* He is indeed handsome. They look at me hopefully. He looks at me hopefully. I continue to pack.

Julia gives me a photo of herself in Italy, leaning on top of a sports car, beaming and sun-swept, every bit the calendar girl. She gives me the photo and asks if I will find her a boyfriend in Australia. I stop packing.

I ask rather naively about her Swiss-Italian sugar hubby. Oh, no, she shakes her head emphatically. "I am free, completely free." She assures me that he has a wife in Switzerland, but shhhhh, the Swiss wife does not know about his Cuban *chica* and *chicleta*. They are *escondidas,* or hidden, which is the same way Cubans describe a large, illicit lobster.

I feel sad. Sad for the wife in Switzerland who bakes her man sugar cookies and rack of lamb, unaware of her sister in the other hemisphere cooking him rice and beans and fried *pargo.*

I give Julia $5.00 and leave them all waving at the front doorstep, waiting for Mr. Eurodaddy to walk up those steps in two weeks' time.

12

CAUGHT

Numerous articles have been written about the illegality of staying in the homes of ordinary Cubans, but after almost a month of thumbing my nose at the rule book, I feel sure that nobody's watching and nobody really cares. I am even getting a little cocky.

The rules for foreigners visiting Cuba are officially thus: Stay in a hotel where Fidel can keep an eye on you, stay out of those quaint-looking old taxicabs, and stay at arm's distance from the locals. The rules for Cubans making whoopee with foreigners are nebulous; *numero uno* is, don't even think about Miami. The only way an ordinary Cuban can travel overseas is by formal invitation from a foreigner, who submits a letter to the Cuban authorities and, naturally, has the capacity and inclination to financially back the exotic visitor.

At the time of this writing, the United States is the only nation that forbids its people from visiting Cuba or, rather, from spending hard currency in that country. But in true American style, where there's a wad to be made, there's a way, and so the U.S. citizen's butt must land in his or her deckchair via an all-inclusive package that many a tour company clamors to promote. It is widely unknown that Cuban immigration merely stamps a piece of paper rather than your passport on entry and exit, making it easy for anyone to pop across from a neighboring country such as Costa Rica.

So amidst more regulations than *Hoyle's Rules of Games,* I set out for Cabo Cruz, a destination to behold for its compelling location at the extreme southwest tip of Granma Province. In my handlebar bag is yet another address supplied by the prolific La China. I head off down the coastal road, looking forward to a new set of welcoming, smiling faces and the open arms to which I have become accustomed.

The road passes by a pleasant and flat beach called Playa Las Coloradas, where Fidel Castro and a force of eighty-one men disembarked from the vessel *Granma* on December 2, 1956. Facing the beach is a *campismo,* a series of small blue concrete cabins joined by narrow concrete paths. I swing past the resort, smug in the knowledge I will soon be making merry in a real Cuban home and not a prefabricated tourist trap.

The road then passes by a park with an attraction of some sort manned by a yawning attendant. I careen past without checking it out. The road soon deteriorates as I get closer to land's end, a small pothole here, a larger one there, then another, spattering the road like the first fat drops of rain before a major downpour, and soon I am weaving around gaping holes strung together by small chunks of pavement.

To increase the difficulty level, the road starts undulating like a serpent's tail, and more than once I mount a sharp rise to have my front wheel wedge into a hole just over the other side. I feel that this stern rite of passage alone makes Cabo Cruz a destination unto itself, a promised land, a holy grail.

A house appears. Then another. I reach a tiny village perched on a cliff that on the map resembles a pizza slice wedged into the raging sea. I descend the steep road, passing more tiny cottages gaily painted like the Cuban equivalent of gingerbread houses, and head toward the lighthouse. Near the base of the lighthouse hulks a concrete building, empty except for a tiny shop that occupies one of the holes in one of the walls. Inside the shop I find a small selection of cream cookies, postcards, and a fridge full of cold drinks. The pretty Cubana behind the counter asks me to write in her tattered notebook some handy English phrases, like "Can I help you?" and "That costs 5 cents" and so on.

I wander outside to sit on the pier and eat the *congris* so generously supplied by Julia, still waiting back in Niquero for her Swiss *esposo*. I watch a few scraggy seagulls circle my lunch spot for stray *congris* and think about how Julia's family would envisage their lives changing if I married her brother. Perhaps they would look forward to becoming a two-television, two-fridge family overnight. Perhaps they would not look forward to paying more for their fresh fish.

The lighthouse is located just short of the tip, which deteriorates into a rocky track and murky-looking swamp. I ask the lighthouse keeper exactly what is beyond the clearing across the way. I want to go to the very end of the road, to the farthest point, like many cyclists who are curiously obsessed with reaching the farthest points on a landmass.

"Is it worth going there?" I ask, not sure I want to immerse my ankles in uncharted puddles.

He moves his hand up and down in a sine-wave fashion.

"*Más o menos,*" he replies. More or less.

I go back and languish on the pier, watching the fishing

boats come and go and bob up and down, enjoying the sensation of being at a land's end in Cuba, comparing how it feels to Land's End in the far southwest of Great Britain, where I started my journey to John O'Groats at the northernmost tip on this same bicycle four years ago.

I feel secure in the knowledge that I have a place to sleep for the night, with good conversation, good food. I can take my time. The tip of the country where I sit is so small that I can throw a rock blindfolded in any direction and probably hit my hosts coming back from a hard day's fishing.

I start feeling a little uneasy at my mounting lethargy and get up to go in search of my host-to-be, Roberto. Someone leads me to his tiny house, back up the hill. The door is open, and from inside the family blinks at me like cave people receiving their first visit from a Kirby vacuum cleaner salesman.

They cautiously listen to me explain how and why I came to Cabo Cruz before they welcome me in. It is the kind of explaining one never has to do at a hotel, and although it can be unsettling, I prefer it because the hospitality I receive is real. Each time I knock at a door with only a scribbled address in hand, I know I am possibly the first and last foreigner to cross their welcome mat. The authenticity excites me.

Roberto is a fisherman, tall and wave-beaten. His muscled wife, Hortensia, looks like she could swing a mean net as well. They are proud people. They tell me that at times, Roberto can make $900 a month selling fish on the black market to support his family of four kids, a phenomenal amount of money for a Cuban.

I park my bike in their living room and wander back down into the town to take some pictures. One of their little girls holds my hand tightly, as if our palms are screwed together. We sit side by side, like mismatched sisters, on the cement seawall. We chat in simple Spanish about life in Cabo Cruz, which for this *chica* is fish and the school building across the road. Her voice is small and piping. At times like this, and only at times like this, my brain reaches into its archives and dusts off a poem I wrote in England, in 1997, when a little girl sat beside me in a car in a nondescript town called Slough.

I put my arm around a little girl to keep her warm
I rub her stockinged legs briskly with my palms
Her bony little shoulders poke through her acrylic shawl
She pipes up and tells me who cuts her hair
Detailed instructions, how to get there from her house
A tiny little voice not often heard
I suddenly think
I want to take you shopping in Slough
I want to walk along the pavement holding your tiny hand
I want to lie with you on your patchwork quilt
Being silly
Just hanging around while you grow a little
Just rubbing your stockinged legs to keep you warm.

We're enjoying the pause of time when her older sister comes down the hill looking concerned. She tells me that there is a policeman back at the house who wants to talk to me.

Oh.

We trudge back up the hill. By the time we reach the house, I have rehearsed the entire confrontation with the policeman in advance, a pleasant and smooth exchange ending with him smiling, tipping his hat, and wandering off out of sight and out of mind. Everything dissolves to stark reality when I see the man in uniform sitting in a chair. He comes straight to the point.

"You cannot stay here."

"Why?"

"Some tanks full of drugs were found floating off the coast near Pilón the other day."

A glance at a map reveals Cabo Cruz to be within straight line-eye contact with Jamaica to the east. A very plausible drug corridor, and no doubt I was a blip on their proverbial drug radar the moment I appeared over the horizon.

"Listen, I don't smoke, I don't snort, and I certainly don't deal," I protest. "I just want to pitch my tent right here in Roberto and Hortensia's front garden for one night."

"You cannot. Anything could happen to you out there, and we would be responsible."

He tells me to return to the *campismo* at Playa Las Coloradas, that it is "proper and appropriate accommodation for tourists."

He is pleasant enough about it. Rather than being a killjoy out to ruin my cultural experience, he is simply doing his job. The government decrees that foreigners must be treated like presidents. Foreigners are the source of the dollar. Everything must be done to ensure that the source of dollars is not endangered in any way.

Thus, my removalist is simply following orders and earning his $20 a month.

"But I take responsibility for myself," I reply with feeling. He shakes his head. I once heard that if a foreigner is insistent enough, even a Cuban policeman will eventually throw up his hands.

But not this one.

I ask for assurance that Roberto and Hortensia will not be in trouble for offering to accommodate me. He assures me that they are not in trouble, though I cannot be sure of what exactly will happen to them after I leave. A Cuban businessman who defected to Miami tells me later that locals offering unauthorized levels of chumminess to foreigners will get a visit from their local authorities, that is, their neighbors, just to make sure they know who's sucking the biggest cigar.

And leave I do, hastily, because it is almost 7:00 P.M. and the sun is sinking over that godforsaken pot-holed road. Hortensia and Roberto plead with me to wait one minute as they furiously fry some fish. They pile my lunch box high with *congris* and press the fish on top. I place it in my pannier and barely express enough gratitude before speeding away.

I arrive back at the deserted *campismo* that I snubbed a few hours ago, and that now looks like a Motel 6 with a light left on for me.

There is just enough dusk left for a quick stroll along the empty, calm beach before darkness falls like an axe. I pedal up the road to find someone who can open up a cabin for me. In one of the houses dotted along the road, I find a young girl with a baby who is supposed to be on duty but has decided to take the night off. She cheerfully opens a cabin, takes my $5.00, and disappears off into the darkness.

I push the bike into the little airless cell with its cold shower, sliding aluminum windows, and large glass door. There are no curtains. This particular *campismo* has been designated as suitable for tourists, so it is clean and presentable, with a tiled floor and a toilet that flushes. In the room are four bunk beds with wafer-thin mattresses. The panes of uncurtained blackness around me make me feel like a beacon, shining out to attract some giant unwelcome visitor on two or more legs. I take the mattress off one of the beds and try to prop it up against the glass door to afford some privacy from no one in particular.

I sit on the bed and open the little lunch box of *congris* and fried fish, still warm from my swift getaway. It is delicious, and with every mouthful I think of Roberto and Hortensia and the little girl who would not let go of my hand.

• • • •

I wake in sunlight to find a couple of platoons of ants marching across the room toward the bin where I have deposited the remains of the fish. The *campismo* is dead quiet. I pack up slowly and leave, asking the man at reception if he can deliver my thank-you note to Roberto and Hortensia, who live over the hill and far away. He tells me that his wife works in Cabo Cruz at different times during the week and she can deliver it. I give him 7 pesos. He might have been telling the truth; it is worth a shot.

Once more I walk the beach that Fidel once walked, then pedal slowly back toward Niquero.

I pop in on Julia, and together we walk down to the square so I can buy a couple more of those killer pizzas and *fongos,* short sweet bananas used for cooking or eating. This time she is somewhat distant, as if all the stops were pulled out for my maiden visit because she wasn't expecting to see me again. A Cuban had told me, "You probably won't write, because all foreigners say they will, and they never do. They never write; they never come back."

I remember a magical trip to Bali some years ago with my ex. We swore we'd be back later that year to whoop it up with a local guide and his wonderful family, who we'd stumbled upon by accident. We took pictures of the children and promised them we'd post them. We never went back. We never sent those pictures. Lack of time and funds seemed to dictate that the effort to keep both promises would be better blown on something brand new and shiny and transient.

A few years later, with life more in perspective, I was able to return to a place in Ireland I had visited before, and the experience was brand new. Rather than shiny, it had a soft glow. I was able to take a second impression. The ground was the same underfoot, but in my mind I had traveled a new road. And it was comforting to find that some people, like my friend Eddie in Cahersiveen and the eccentric Peter in his Waterville hostel, had not moved—that part of my world was intact. People with less have less luxury to get dissatisfied and up and leave; their world is more limited to their immediate vicinity, which means their bonds with it run deep. These bonds are vapid or nonexistent in a faster, disposable society that offers more choices, distractions, and room for dissatisfaction. In colonized countries like America and Australia, the effect is magnified by the lack of roots reaching back farther than colonial history, the absence of a truly *ancient* history. This must be why cultures like Cuba's and Nicaragua's feel as familiar and welcoming to me as an old family friend, even after just one visit. But, later, landing in mainstream America— rather, the twenty-six-aisle megamart grocery store—felt like landing on Mars without a street map.

I say good-bye to Julia for probably the last time, and she gives me the address of a friend in Holguín. She repeats her request for an Australian boyfriend. She is already turning away as I pack my pizza and *fongos* in my handlebar bag and then pedal away, watching her become smaller and smaller in my rearview mirror.

Behind me, a waiting woman. In front of me, about 35 kilometers north, the coastal town of Media Luna, or half moon.

13

THE 55-CENT HOTEL

I've ridden constantly for a week and a half without a decent rest day, and now I notice some engine trouble. I am starting to run out of puff around 2:00 P.M. each day, regardless of what I pour into my tank. I experienced this phenomenon when cycling through Britain four years ago. When I got to the top of Scotland, my gut was pierced by a dull ache that would wax and wane, with sufficient gaps between surprise attacks to keep me from doing something concrete about it, like visiting a doctor. I'd feel great one minute, lousy the next.

When I finally got to Inverness, the low-grade pain was on my mind constantly, so I took myself to a hospital and waited several hours to be told they could find nothing conclusive. The young intern seemed more fascinated about my travelogue, which I dispensed in *Reader's Digest* condensed form between gritted teeth; it was probably the only time I resented telling my tales.

I heard one doctor say that sometimes the best medicine is a dose of time. The body deals with things when it is ready and not before. Hearing this may have had a subconscious effect, because my gut problem cleared up in due course. I only noticed it had gone when I realized I hadn't thought about it for quite some time.

The road to Media Luna is hard and headwindy. I pant my way there with half my pistons firing. But I make it. Actually, I want to go farther, but my stomach bug is coming along for the ride.

The little hotel in the main street is full of delegates attending a conference. I look at the crumbling shack of a hotel and wonder what kind of conference. The proprietor tells me that there are cabins for rent on the beach, which I locate with some difficulty.

At first I am refused in the usual way ("it's full"), but further pleading leads to a heavy sigh and scratching of unshaven chin by the very handsome but humorless attendant. He repeats several times that he is not authorized to rent to foreigners; finally he caves in to my pleas. He reminds me of that ruggedly hunky monster in *Reservoir Dogs* who had a penchant for slicing off ears, and I muse momentarily about how life rattles its dice: Mr. Famous Ear Slicer actor is probably languishing beside a pool somewhere, smoking Cuban cigars and wondering whether to order salmon or caviar on his bagel, while his body double is languishing here in this concrete cubicle, cogitating about renting a cabin to a vagabond on a bike.

The "resort" consists of a run-down block of two dank, concrete "suites," each with a nonfunctioning shower cubicle. The rack rate is 11.30 pesos (about 55 cents) a night. On casual inspection it strikes me that the only thing missing from the room is the central torture table. Out on the beach, equally tragic A-frame cabins rent for 16.30 pesos a night (80 cents), each barely lit by an unflattering fluorescent light.

At first the attendant shows me to the hotel block, no doubt well-meaning in wanting to give me the most economical room. After pacing the crazed cement floor several times, I decide to upgrade to the luxury of one of the A-frame cabins. However, after enlisting the attendant to help me shift my bags over, I wish I hadn't moved; the windows cannot be opened, there is an air conditioner on the wall that exhales bad breath, and the seatless toilet reeks of stale pee. He shows me how to turn on the light: You flick the switch on the wall, walk to the center of the room, grab the two frayed wires dangling down, and touch them together. The lamp sputters to life. To turn it off, you must use the switch. To turn it on again, you use the two-wire method.

I change into my swimsuit for a celebration dip under the sinking sun and am immediately besieged by mosquitoes and sand flies. I quickly give up after getting only my ankles wet. Besides, the Cuban winter has arrived. In this deserted and condemned holiday spot (someone local tells me that it has a Cuban zero-star rating), I meet a foursome from Bayamo, a town several days away to the northeast that I will duly pass through on my way to Holguín. There's André, an Afro-Cuban; his neighbor; and two giggling Cubanas, also "neighbors," I imagine. They immediately give me their addresses and say that they expect to see me at either of their houses in two days. They are drinking from a bottle of strong stuff, and it occurs to me that they'll probably forget their invitation and blink at me blankly if ever I do land on their doorstep.

They suddenly decide to pile into their rusty old car with its government worker's plates to return to their hometown 160 kilometers inland. They invite me to join them. I decline.

I am walking back to my cabin when a toothless old ice-cream seller appears, his coolbox mounted on the front of his bicycle. He speaks reasonable English, being one of the few who clearly paid attention in class. Absurdly, his passion is not ice-cream flavors but advertising slogans, and he can recite an endless list of them and even come up with new ones.

The only sanctioned advertising in Cuba is government propaganda. But the ice cream man's slogan collection comes from the odd foreign magazine left lying around wherever he dispenses his wares. I ask why he doesn't create a slogan for each of his ice-cream flavors, and his eyes light up. He glares at me intently through the single thick lens in his eyeglass frame, and through that monocular window I glimpse a soaring Madison Avenue mind that was instead born on José Street, Media Luna, Cuba.

Later, I wander over to see what the resort restaurant offers. There is a plate of *congris,* a plate of boiled plantain slices, and a plate of lettuce that comes to 2.80 pesos, or 15 cents. I share my table with a group of three women who are doing some government testing of mosquitoes in the area. One of them shows me a small corked test tube with a single fat mosquito in it. The pages in front of them are wordy and technical. I get out my stashed pizza to share, which the cook generously warms up for me.

I return to my cabin and notice how stuffy it is with the windows closed. I look for the attendant and ask if I may borrow the rickety old fan I saw in the cheaper hotel room. He looks troubled. Apparently the fan is authorized for use in that room only. I point out that he can have it back at 8:00 A.M., before the even bigger boss arrives. He relents, though he is clearly bothered by this flouting of the rule book. I inspect the sheets. They look and smell clean. I fall asleep to the turbo-prop sound of the fan.

In the night I hear a rustling sound. It's the kind of noise that makes your eyes instantly peel open and scan the darkness for a shape you don't want to see.

It stops, then starts again as I am falling back asleep. I reach for the flashlight I put under my pillow when traveling and shine it around the room. The rustling stops. I close my eyes. The rustling starts. I swing the flashlight toward the sound again but see nothing. I close my eyes, glad that I have hung my string bag full of food from the top of the rocking chair.

In the morning I find that the night thief has done a tightrope act of the most daredevil order. All of the *fongos* in the string bag have been neatly split open and the insides nibbled clean. Nothing else has been disturbed. If I catch that rat, I will sell it to Ringling Brothers.

I present the evidence to the attendant, who rubs his unshaven chops, shrugs, and says, "*Eso es Cuba.*" That's Cuba.

• • • •

The road north is buffeted by a strong headwind. To turn the cranks becomes a major effort. I look for a place with a toilet. Or specifically, a house where I can ask to use one. I am not sure what subconscious flowchart my brain uses for the selection process, but seeing a friendly face out in the front garden helps. In a small village called San Ramón, I pass a house with a tiny orchard on the side and a tall boy leaning on a shovel. He smiles and waves. Brake. Stop. Turn around.

Amauris shows me to the "toilet," which is basically the family shower. He motions for me to aim carefully and then goes off to get a bucket of water to flush my efforts. There is a preliminary screening with hand movements and *pissss* noises to determine whether I need to do that kind or the other kind of toilet, and I thank my lucky rune stones I only need to do *that* kind.

Meanwhile, his whole family happily emerges. A couple of small stools are brought out to the garden. I am motioned into one, and their delightful *abuelita* (grandmother) perches herself on another and presents me with a *bocadito* (little snack), a toasted bread roll with lettuce and a flour fritter. I accept the gift with shy gratitude, temporarily trashing my strict lifelong rule about not eating anything deep fried, white, or creamy, an easy-to-remember diet regimen recommended by a friend who studies these things. "If you're traveling, you haven't got room for diet books," she said. "A sentence weighs zip."

I actually enjoy letting go of these mustabations even more than the delicious savory chewiness of the fritter. I comment on how difficult it is to obtain cyclist food, namely bread rolls and bananas, and immediately I am handed six ripe yellow crescents from the family's banana tree and three bread rolls. Of course, to refuse these gifts once I have so coyly solicited them is, as usual, an exercise in futility. I manage to get Amauris to accept a dollar to buy something for his grandma, who reminds me of my late Nanna, right down to the dark sunspots on her cheek and wisps of gray hair where the dye didn't take.

They tell me I must come back in March, when the air is filled with the sweet aroma of plump, fermenting mangoes, and go to the local disco with Amauris. I notice that he has nailed a couple of chrome strips to the heels of his work boots as decoration, giving him a London bovver-boy look without paying for the Doc Martens label. Once a fashion slave, I note that this simple skinhead-style alteration gives him some serious street cred, and I realize the absurd amounts of money that we, the privileged, shell out in the name of fashion.

For a moment I contemplate pitching my tent under their

Edenic mango tree. I finally tear myself away.

Barely 10 kilometers farther on, I stop in a neat little town called Campechuela for a 2-peso pizza (the cheapest yet) and a cone of shelled peanuts. The cone is made from a page torn from a book about health during pregnancy. The pizza is delivered in a couple of pages torn from a Russian–Spanish dictionary.

"So, you're not interested in learning Russian?" I ask the lad tossing the pizzas.

The tongue-in-cheek question draws cackles of laughter from the crowd that has gathered, as always, around my bike and me.

Cuba is still a communist country, and while muttering under their breath about things needing to change, the people by and large have a great deal of pride in their heritage and what their government stands for. However, for at least this young entrepreneur, learning the language of Russian comrade nations is no longer lucrative or meaningful. People are waiting in lines here, too, but at least it's for his pizza.

As I wait at least three people level the two usual questions at me: "Do you have children? Are you married?"

No, and no.

"Why?"

I shrug.

I eat my peanuts, and I am observed intently by many pairs of half-closed eyes. Nobody seems in a hurry to be anywhere at any particular time. When the last peanut is gone, I unfurl the page that they were wrapped in and very seriously start reading aloud, as if reading a fortune from a fortune cookie, about nutrition during pregnancy. The observers smile and cackle.

They are all part of a family, a family that can share and laugh at such a quiet joke—*la familia, la familia de Fidel*. Without the opportunities and placations of a material world, family is one thing that Cubans can and do strive for. No matter how poor or disillusioned, wretched or enlightened, almost every Cuban has someone to go home to, whether it's a family of their own making or someone else's. Almost every Cuban belongs; almost every Cuban would be missed at a dinner table.

Cuba, not Australia, may well be the lucky country.

14

A SEEMINGLY SACRED PLACE

Manzanillo, Manzanillo. *Mahn-zahn-knee-yo.* The little town of Manzanillo is important to me for the inane reason that it has the same name as the village in Costa Rica where my Dutch beau lives. If I can make it to just one place in Cuba, that place must be Manzanillo.

Jungle Boy, as I affectionately call him, lives in a circular house in the rainforest canopy on the Caribbean coast of Costa Rica. At daybreak the large, unscreened bedroom windows of his house are a moving mural of monkeys, parrots, and sloths hanging from a thick curtain of dripping vines and mossy trunks. Each day breaks with a distinct pattern of sounds: the guttural *croak, croak, croak* of howler monkeys; the *pew, pew, pewing* of a bird I can't name; the *bzzzzzz* of a zillion bitey things; and the *shwoooosh* of fronds the size of surfboards as something snares its breakfast. Ten minutes down the dusty road, the sea washes the coconut-strewn shore. There is little to do but plant tropical flowers, take a lukewarm dip in the ocean, and swing in the hammock while browsing coffee-table books in Dutch.

Manzanillo, Manzanillo.

I am photographing the name on billboards, street signs, and patriotic posters shouting MANZANILLO EN COMBATE (Manzanillo at War). I spend a long time setting up a self-timer photo of me next to the sign leading into the town. Manzanillo, Manzanillo. I sing the name out loud.

Manzanillo turns out to be a faded and chipped old port town with a long *malecón* that skirts the edge of the bay. There is a salty, forgotten taste in the air. The narrow streets rise steeply up a hill to meet a ridge where a memorial to Celia Sánchez Manduley, Castro's lover and muse, perches at the top of a long, gradual stairway. Celia lived in Manzanillo during the Revolution and helped rally support for the army that was building in the Sierra Maestra. After the war she remained a top confidante of Fidel and a leader in the Cuban women's movement. The memorial is a series of tiled concrete monoliths inscribed with large yellow sunflowers painted in relief.

La China from El Uvero has given me the cryptic address of her brother in Manzanillo. As always happens when I am staring at a flapping map turned the wrong way on a windy street corner, someone approaches and asks if I need help. Quite often I politely decline, partly because it does nothing to improve my map reading and congenitally bad sense of direction.

This time, a man named José stops and asks all the usual questions, to which I give all the usual answers. Then he offers to take me to his house to meet his wife and, later, to the address I am looking for. It is early.

José and María share a little house up on a hill behind a sports center. They are not married, and for the first time in Cuba I find myself standing in the house of a couple where there are no childish voices in the kitchen. Both are divorcés, now living quite well on their combined and unencumbered incomes. He earns $25 a month as a transport supervisor driver; she earns $15 a month working in a store.

He is the only Cuban I meet who openly states that life in Cuba is good, a viewpoint he attributes to childlessness. Their house is comfortably furnished with lacy curtains, crockery cabinets, and worn but plump sofas. There is a small and newish-looking television on a table, and I guess that it is color.

• • • •

A bicycle appears at the gate. It is José's brother, Danilo, a deaf mute since birth. This has not deterred him from holding down a job, regularly traveling 25 kilometers on his bicycle to visit his brother, and having a willing woman waiting for him at home each night.

He sits down, and José explains to Danilo, with a series of silent and efficient gestures, how I, a small Australian with a *China* face riding a small wheeled bicycle, came to be sitting in his house.

First, he makes a fist and bounces it in the air to denote a kangaroo. Then an airplane gesture with his arms signifies how I came to Cuba. Fists rotating beside each other denote my mode of travel, a bicycle. He wipes his hand across his forehead to indicate the hard pedaling I am enduring. Two hands with fingers touching in a pyramid shape, followed by closed eyes, shows how I sleep at night, when not otherwise accommodated, in a small tent. A hand waving in the air means I am heading off into the wild blue yonder.

I embellish this account in similar sign language, amazed and gratified when Danilo understands immediately and totally. The conversation is silent but full.

Danilo suddenly gets up and makes an hourglass shape with his hands, which means either that his hour is up or that someone that shape is awaiting his return. He disappears with a thumb's-up sign.

• • • •

Later, José accompanies me on a walk along the seafront. I mention that I like vanilla ice cream; as a result he keeps leading me into dark, seedy-looking bars. I soon figure out, from the furtive way he pronounces the word *vanilla,* that he is mistaking vanilla ice cream for some mischievous alcoholic cocktail that sounds like it.

We eventually land on the same page and stop at a Coppelia ice-cream bar. All the while I wonder what is going on in his head. My mild paranoia is somewhat tempered by the timid and gentle face of María, his *novia* (girlfriend), waiting back home in the kitchen.

In the evening I help her prepare the meal. It includes a decent proportion of meat; though there is plenty to go around, I stick to my rice and beans and cabbage.

The next morning, as I am packing, José asks if I have a memento he could remember me by. In my quest to take only hospitality and leave only goodwill plus a few dollars, I cannot find a single worthwhile object in my belongings to give him.

I try to explain my minimalist travel philosophy, but somehow it sounds lame. I give a $5.00 bill to María when José is not looking. Is that what he means by memento? I'm not sure.

• • • •

I coast down toward the sea and find the house of La China's brother, Jorge. His is a tall, faded door with a small, tightly sealed window and three tiny steps anchoring it to the pavement. I knock with a coin. The square peephole slides open to frame a cheerful face with smiling eyes and a mop of dark curls—La China's sister-in-law, Zaida.

More introductions, patient nodding, more smiles. The door unbolts, and I go inside. As I schlep my panniers into her living room, I think about doing this someplace outside Cuba, landing on someone's welcome mat in suburbia with a scribbled address on a scrap of toilet paper. . . . How welcome would I be?

Zaida and Jorge's house is like Dr. Who's Tardis. The small aperture of a front door opens into a deceptively large tiled room with a churchlike hush. Tall, flaking columns join at the ceilings in arches with faint murals, an elegant ruin. The roof disappears abruptly in the center of the house, creating an impromptu courtyard. Large steel drums stand in a line under the open sky to collect rainwater as a backup for the once-a-week supply through the pipes.

At age thirty-six Zaida is already a grandmother, and she bounces her little granddaughter on her knee as we talk. Life is hard work (she wipes the side of her forefinger across her forehead). Her husband is a crop supervisor and is on the road most of each week. She cooks me a meal of rice and beans with some fried fish.

I ride down to a bakery at the other end of town and, putting my head around the side entrance, ask to buy a few rolls. A woman with a troubled face is sweeping water off the path outside the bakery. She sweeps agitatedly, now and then lashing out at people waiting for the bakery to open in half an hour or so. On hearing of my request, she proclaims loudly that foreigners are not permitted to buy bread from the *bodega*. A young man standing nearby approaches me and asks if I want to wait inside his house opposite the bakery and meet his family. He explains that he is a former employee there.

Marco's house is a hollowed-out concrete shell that he shares with his pregnant wife, two small children, aunt, niece, and nephew all crammed into one small room. They make me coffee, sweet and black and rich, the universal Cuban language of welcome. His wife, a warm and gentle girl, pulls out a tattered exercise book. She explains that she listens to the radio for broadcast addresses of the many foreigners who want a Cuban pen pal.

She has written letters to many of them but has never received a reply. Her young husband ducks out and returns with about a dozen soft and warm bread rolls, given to him *gratis* by ex-colleagues. I hold out a dollar to pay for them, but the payment is flatly refused.

"All I ask is that you write to my wife," he says. He points to my ballpoint pen and indicates that it would be a far more useful gift.

I promise to write. Her address is Arismilda Reyes Cintra, Martí #41 between Tomas Barrero and San Silvestre, Manzanillo, Granma, CUBA, 87510.

• • • •

I wander back to Zaida's house the long way, by the *malecón,* with the perpetual ocean breeze sweeping up the streets toward the monument to Celia Sánchez Manduley. I pass by a cart selling ham rolls for 12 pesos, with mustard.

A large, juicy leg of ham sits in the small glass case, its

carved side pink and inviting. I do not eat ham, but it looks good. I can only deduce that after a steady diet of rice and beans and cabbage salad for the past few weeks, even a shish kebab of breaded frogs' larynxes would look good—so why not a slice of juicy, red ham? I buy one, noting pointlessly to myself that it cost 4 pesos more than the best pizza in Cuba, the one I ate three of in Niquero. It is salty and tasty, and I enjoy it without thinking of how long it has been gazing out of that case.

Jorge will not return for a few days yet. Zaida pleads with me to stay and meet her husband, but something unsentimental is edging me on.

I've smelled the sweat of hard-working people, the comforting aroma of fresh-baked bread, the gentle sadness of the Celia Sánchez shrine. Now the breeze is sweeping me northward, away from Manzanillo.

15

GUANTANAMERA

I haven't pedaled very far before I notice a peculiar gnawing feeling in the pit of my stomach. The gnawing now escalates into an all-out feeding frenzy, sending daggers of pain through my abdomen and slapping leg irons on my ankles.

Bocadito belly? I am almost sure of it. I curse my weakening to the forbidden ham. To make matters worse, the headwind is hard as a wall and the road as straight as Australia's empty, lonely Nullabor Desert Highway, and nowhere near as scenic. All in all, perfect conditions to request a ride. I pull over and wait, hoping I don't faint from the food fight now in full swing inside my Lycra bike shorts.

A tractorlike vehicle slowly approaches, its engine rat-a-tatting. It grinds its way to a halt before me, and a chubby mustachioed driver jumps out. Hitched to the back of the tractor is a metal trailer with high crate walls lined with rice sacks. I decide that a woman in my condition is in no position to be choosy, so I let him throw the bike, panniers, and me into the trailer, where I look for a decent handhold. There isn't one. The driver asks if I would mind a short detour so he can deliver a package to a friend's farm. As of four years ago, my whole life has been a detour, so I see no reason to object.

As we hammer along the highway, the trailer sways and skids and seems to repeatedly part company from the tractor, as if towed with a piece of tired old elastic. I clutch at the rice sacks in vain, totally unable to see over the top, which makes it feel like I've crawled into some condemned ride in an abandoned fun fair and a mysterious hand has thrown the switch. I spread my feet for stability, watching my bike and bags slide and scrape around, glad that I'd pragmatically chosen black—which can be touched up with a magic marker—for the color of my bike. The ride soon becomes particularly bumpy, and I sense that we are crossing, if not ploughing, a field. Finally, we come to a halt, and I realize that I've forgotten all about my stomach troubles. I throw open the crate door and make for the tiny passenger seat beside the driver for the remainder of the ride.

The view from the tractor cabin is better, but the sound is deafening. I believe that the driver, stocky and jocular, is saying something about his wife stabbing one of their children to death before stabbing herself and, by the way, would I like to come and stay at his house?

I scream a polite decline, partly because I have an address to go to: the address of André from Bayamo, whom I had met on the beach of the banana-rat hotel in Media Luna. He and his friends invited me to come and stay, and I am taking them up on their kind offer, even though it was probably done under the influence of alcohol.

The driver drops me off on the outskirts of Bayamo, and I check that all the bolts on my bike are sound before consulting the map.

Bayamo is a melancholy city with run-down neighborhoods

and little else. It appears to have no redeeming features other than a very pleasant, shady central square. André and his family live on the edge of town in a grid of narrow dirt streets lined with houses that parch in the sun. As I gingerly pick my way through the neighborhood, returning the stares from all around, it becomes clear that no outsider has successfully conducted business here, personal or otherwise, and probably never will.

I locate André's house, an upstairs cube of a small two-story duplex. He emerges from above; now stone-cold sober, he seems taken aback that I have actually followed through on his offer of a room for the night. I always say to people: Beware of offering an Aussie hospitality; we're likely to say yes. Sensing his hesitation, I quickly tell him that I can go elsewhere, but he reassures me that there is no problem and leads me upstairs.

He shares this compact space with his wife, María, and two teenage boys. I am given one of the boy's beds, which María immediately makes up with clean sheets. I am the first *extranjera* ever to visit his house, says André. I am almost sure of that. He asks his eldest boy to take me into town and show me the sights. At this point I note the ceasefire in my stomach and accept the invitation with gusto.

We start walking down the road and take one of the horse-drawn carriages clopping by. As we bounce down the highway and along the main approach, I sense that I am entering a place that will not appear in any glossy guidebook. Bayamo is a forgotten city, desperate and dirty, one giant tooting, ringing, whinnying traffic jam of old cars, old horses, rusty bikes, muddy potholes, and people wandering around with trays selling small morsels of food—a place where the same kinds of daily transactions and interactions are taking place as in the finest cities in the world, but no one would know it, much less care.

. . . .

As I sit on a park bench, I converse with André's two boys in my broken Spanish. They are at school and want to be engineers. They are nice boys, polite, insisting on paying for the horse-and-cart ride. At that moment nausea envelops me. *Bocadito* belly has decided to stage a comeback. I tell the boys I must return to the house immediately. I can barely hold out in the carriage.

When we get back to the house, a meal is ready on the table, a place set like a shrine for the VIP visitor. I have to gently turn it down after two nibbles, and with much apologizing and bowing, I find my way to the bed and collapse. I lie there whimpering until I remember the antideath tablets from Australia that I always carry with me when traveling. Noroxin (which does not carry the slogan "Kills everything but you," but should) saved me in Nepal several years ago when, after eating something at the "five-star" hotel in Pokhara, I came down with a gut ache so debilitating that I could not even raise my head to get my trekking-pass photograph taken. Two tablets restored me to singing-dancing-wisecracking life within twenty-four hours. I pull out the medicine and take two.

I sleep spasmodically, woken by the intermittent bursts of *la novela* from the television. Through the thin curtain the glow is eclipsed by the large, black planetary mass that is André in his favorite chair.

I open my eyes a lifetime later, check to see that I am still of this world, and discover that *bocadito* belly has laid down its arms. I cautiously rise and prepare to leave.

"When you come back to Cuba, come back here," sing André and his neighborhood watch.

This is the most common farewell statement I encounter in

Cuba. I finish packing my bike out front, in the dusty lane, where the usual crowd of onlookers has gathered. I want to give André some money, but with fifteen pairs of eyes upon us, I think better of it and make an excuse to bolt back upstairs. María is in the kitchen. I hug her and press $5.00 into her hand. She protests. I give her another hug and slide back down to ground level and my farewell throng.

When you come back to Cuba, come back here. I am struck with a sad and final feeling that I probably will not be coming back.

I head for Holguín, the city of curiously golden-haired, blue-eyed Cubans. The road is dead flat, dead long, and deadly frustrating because of the persistent headwind that insists on poking a big fat finger into my chest no matter which way I turn. I pull over several times to flop down on the stony verge and recuperate.

During one of these pit stops, I meet a couple on a motorcycle who are having intermittent engine trouble. He taps away at something with a wrench, and we chat a little before they putt-putt off. A while later I come across them again, tapping away with the wrench. They manage to start, but the engine falters again just a few meters ahead.

Several more stops like this, and we know each other's recent life histories. They give me their address and insist that I come and stay. In a reflective moment it occurs to me that only with several meetings can trust and friendship be developed. I remember meeting a fellow cyclist in a hostel in Ireland; we began a breathless and animated conversation that lasted a solid two hours standing at the kitchen door. We had absolutely nothing more to say to each other after that, not even on e-mail. The cup was full. Had we poured too fast? With gradual filling there is a chance to stop and sip and savor, and to ask for a little more each time. Gulping the entire kettleful left us sated. Is it the pauses, not the parties, that create friendship?

• • • •

The road slices through flat farmland and does not wiggle for the entire 75 kilometers. I hallucinate in the strong sunlight about cruise control for bicycles, and I almost have it designed and patented by the time I enter the outskirts of Holguín. I barely make it to the house of Juan Carlos, a friend of Julia back in Niquero, before my legs give out.

Juan Carlos lives in a triangular stone house with a walled garden on the corner of a cobbled street. He shares it with his pregnant second wife, Yame; his stalwart mother, Dulce María; and, on certain days, his daughter from his first marriage. Juan Carlos has not worked for two months because of a kidney operation, so the government pays him half his salary, or about 100 pesos a month, roughly $5.00. The perks of his job as a steward in an expensive hotel in Guardalavaca are clearly in evidence: a Daewoo color television, a video recorder, Nike tennis shoes, and Swatch watches. But, as I soon discover, none of these items is edible.

Dinner is to be rice, beans, eggs, and cabbage as well as a tiny chicken leg that we agree will be given to Yame and her ravenous unborn. Chattering amiably, Juan Carlos reaches for one of the two empty plastic cooking-oil bottles on the sink. He squeezes it, and it wheezes dry air.

"What a pity," he says, cheerfully popping it back on the windowsill, as if discovering that someone has merely taken the last Oreo cookie out of a packet rather than an entire meal for four and a half persons.

At this point I pull out a $10 bill. Usually, I would make my offering at the end of a stay, for all kinds of reasons, including not embarrassing my hosts, but now seems like a good and useful time.

"Lynette, what is that for?" asks Juan Carlos. Dulce María's black eyes burn silently. He refuses the money. It is not difficult to change his mind.

"Come," he says and grabs my hand. He scoops up his daughter, and we step outside the house, locking the gate in the high wall.

A couple of doors down we pass a *bufete colectivo,* a large practice of lawyers where one can get married, get divorced, or settle a dispute. We joke that I can get married then and there to a passerby and spend the rest of my days in Cuba. The serious part is that I can so quickly and easily make that joke a reality.

With this lightbulb burning in my brain, I glance across the road and see a sign: *HOGAR DE ABUELITOS DESEMPARADOS*—literally, "Home for Discarded Old Grandparents." It is a retirement home where the few Cubans who somehow managed to miss out on having a warm and loving family in this warm and loving society can prepare to meet their maker with, perhaps, a hand to hold as they go. Juan tells me that the incumbents receive pocket money, good food, love, and care from volunteers in the community and even pleasant beach vacations, all at the government's expense. I reflect on how the introduction of this freebie back home would lead to a stampede to offload infirm and incontinent grannies and grandpappies. Here in Cuba, it is seen as a poor and sorry alternative to a true family environment, even if the latter is without the free beach vacations and soft pillows and meals always cooked with fresh and plentiful cooking oil.

••••

About a block farther down the street we step into a sleek dollar shop where Juan buys oil, a packet of spaghetti, a tin of tomato salsa, and ice cream for his daughter. He clearly wants me to see that my gift is put to good use and not squandered. It reminds me of La China in El Uvero and Zaida in Manzanillo, both of whom insisted that they would write and tell me exactly what they had bought with my gift. I told them to buy what they liked and realized that they would look at that money in a very different way than I would.

Back at the house, the new supplies and chicken leg enable Dulce María to prepare dinner for us after all. She pours the *pru,* a dark, fermented concoction made by soaking a handful of tree bark and a wild root called *yuca india,* dug up from the surrounding woods, in a bucket of water for a few days. The *pru* ferments; then the heady tonic is strained and chilled in discarded plastic soda bottles. It is delicious and refreshing, apparently good for digestion, and tastes of carbonated dark iced tea mixed with fragrant wood shavings. Dulce María tells me that it is a specialty of the old wives of the Oriente, meaning that one would be unlikely to find it in Havana. I entertain the inevitable future vision of shiny Pru-Up cans barreling out of big red vending machines.

Dulce is a stout woman of fifty hard and harrowing years and has the resolve and countenance of an ox. With dark eyes blazing she tells me how her husband suicidally threw himself into a well and died when Juan was barely four years old. She flops around in a pair of rubber thongs and admires the cheap strap sandals I bought in Costa Rica at the last minute for swimming and beach walking. I want to give them to her, but I need this piece of equipment lest I step on an infectious spike, as I did once in Costa Rica. I weakly resolve to send them to her when I leave.

"Tomorrow we will go and find water and milk," she says.

••••

It is evening, and I am writing in my diary.

Juan Carlos calls out to me to come and watch a "very good" video on the big Daewoo screen. The video is a documentary on the many recent classroom shootings that have taken place in the United States. I note how intently the family take in the distressed and teary faces of children recounting the horror of seeing their classmates blown to shreds. The video must have been issued by someone who wanted to make sure that Cubans continue to believe that, despite holes in their jeans and a single bread roll per day, they are actually the lucky ones. It is the only video in the house.

I step outside and stroll toward the town square in the balmy night. The streets are quiet. "¡Cuidado!" (be careful), implores Dulce María. She insists on waiting up for me. I choose to wear my long black dress with no pockets for money or keys.

I am drawn to music emanating from a rooftop. Down below, the doorman of the nightclub says I must pay $1.00 to enter, but I have not brought any cash with me.

"Sin bolsas, sin problemas" (no pockets, no problems), I reply, pulling out the sides of my dress. He waves me upstairs.

On the roof is a discotheque playing obscure rock music. A group of tipsy young students surrounds me and introduces themselves. One of the boys, named Carlos, tells me what a terrible country Cuba is.

"No freedom to choose," he laments. His father is a professor but apparently is not free to dictate his own curriculum. Carlos then pulls out a ringing mobile phone.

I return to the main square, a majestic quadrangle of colonial arches from which numerous dollar stores operate. The local supermarket is stacked high with dollar goods, including fancy cookies for $1.50 a packet. To bring one of these back to Juan Carlos's house would be like bringing home a giant black forest ganache from a high street patisserie.

I get back at 10:00 P.M. Dulce María has been mildly fretting for my safety. She pulls out my bed, a white tubular plastic sun lounge that Juan begged, borrowed, or stole from the resort where he worked. We drag it into the kitchen, the only available space, and spread it with towels as impromptu bedding. I wrestle with the poor ergonomics of this contraption for quite some time before drifting off to the loud snoring of Dulce María in the curtained room next door.

The next morning I wake to find the family tiptoeing around me. They make my favorite breakfast, a bread roll with a banana pressed inside and squashed in a heated waffle iron. I wonder if this could evolve to a standard *bocadito* in Cuba and become known as *Chinitas*, the staple of some strange China-Australiana on a folding bicycle who ventured here a long, long time ago. In the courtyard outside Dulce María is loading up a wire trolley with three very large plastic containers.

"We are going to get water now," she explains.

We trundle down the streets, turning this way and that, with Juan's portly daughter leading the way. Dulce María stops to greet practically everyone who crosses her path. I think of opposing streams of ants, each ant gently touching feelers with an oncoming ant over and over and over. She stops to talk to an old man, and I hear him say that he knows where to acquire some milk for the toddler, and that he will get it for her. She gives him an empty Sprite bottle.

We finally stop outside a store that has nothing inside but three large tubes trailing out the door and a bored attendant behind an empty desk. Water, clean pure drinking water, cheap at 20 centavos, or 1 cent, for each of our three enormous plastic tanks. Dulce María unscrews the caps from the containers, and we begin filling, filling, filling. When all three tanks are full, I cannot move the trolley. Dulce María simply throws her momentous frame against the handlebar, and the trolley moves forward. I help her push it along, but judging from the lack of pressure on my hands, I know she needs no help. She has done this many times before.

On the way back we encounter the undercover milkman, who produces her Sprite bottle half filled with milk.

"This we will dilute with water," says Dulce María, tapping on one of the tanks. I do some impromptu grocery shopping and manage to score a free cabbage, a cucumber, four bread rolls, and some homemade biscotti that puts the packet variety imported from Italy to shame. These *regalos* are not from my haggling, but from simply reaching into my pocket to fumble clumsily for pesos or trying to pay in dollars when they only want pesos. They smile and say "*un regalo.*" A gift. Despite the seductive allure of the dollar, many Cubans outside Havana and the tourist zones are still more comfortable buying and selling in their own currency.

Later, Dulce María takes me to visit a secure children's park where kids are allowed to commit acts with small plastic bicycles that they would not try at home, while parents watch from shaded benches. A man approaches, selling what I soon discover to be the perfect cycling food: *panqueque*. This chewy, spicy slice resembles a peanut butter and honey PowerBar without the fancy packaging and is super-cheap at a peso a slab. Dulce María tells me that it is given to schoolchildren for free and that she will take me to where the product is made so that I might stock up to my carb's content.

• • • •

We walk several blocks until we reach a building that looks like a workshop of some sort with the door broken off. The home of *panqueque*. Out front sit a woman typing on a manual typewriter and a man who is filling out papers. It's their outdoor office. Dulce María explains our quest. They shrug.

"None today. There is no gasoline to run the ovens."

The man looks at me closely.

"*Extranjera?*" he asks Dulce María. She nods and explains how I am cycling around Cuba, embellishing her account with kangaroo and airplane charades. He holds up both palms.

"*Espérate, espérate*" (wait, wait), he says, and disappears inside. He emerges with a box of *panqueque,* just a few pieces, and motions me to take all I want. He refuses payment.

"Cubans like to help foreigners as much as possible," says Dulce María as we wander home with our booty, noting my slight guilt about my free gifts. "And whenever a Cuban says there isn't any, a little explanation is all it takes for them to say '*Espérate, espérate,*' and suddenly things appear."

That evening we watch more Elián protests on the television. This time three full hours are devoted to a woman reading sections of the law governing the kidnapping of minors in other countries such as Canada and Italy. I thought of donning my *SALVEMOS A ELIÁN* T-shirt for the occasion, but that would feel phony. What would I know anyway? How would life in Cuba compare to life in the States for a little Cuban boy, for whom simple parental love may be more important than the latest download of *Tomb Raider?* Having lived in neither the States nor Cuba, and with no children of my own, I feel I lack a frame of reference.

• • • •

Day three in Holguín. My cycling legs are returning, but instead of jumping on the bike I decide to tackle La Loma de la Cruz, a conspicuous tor that stands on the northern edge of town. This curious hill resembles the hump of a very large camel. A striking feature is the dead-straight, 430-step stairway that connects the ground to the summit like a ladder and that is almost as vertical. A road gently winds its way round the hill's girth and finishes at a parking lot at the top.

The vertical ascent requires me to take several stops to catch my breath and rest on the thoughtfully placed benches along the way. Moses going up or down the mountain comes to mind. At the top is a large grassy area with a retaining wall all round and a small souvenir shop. The 360-degree view takes in all of Holguín and the outlying urban areas. Farther toward the north is a ring of hills beyond which lies the tourist playground of Guardalavaca.

A couple of mustachioed *trovadores* (musicians) are serenading the tourist buses that periodically chug up the road to disgorge their white-sneakered camera-danglers and wait while dollar notes are exchanged for seed necklaces before whisking them back down the mountain. Only I am left behind, one of the flotsam outside the clean, highly organized, and mechanized tourist trade. When the crooning, strumming pair has collected their month's rent, I ask to borrow one of the guitars.

We sit together in the shade and sing one of the sad travel songs I wrote while in Costa Rica. The two men understand not a word but listen as if they understand everything, nodding at the sad parts, smiling at the glad part, which is actually sadder than the rest. There is a sadness in the music of the *trovador,* his gentle notes falling on the often cynical and impatient ear of the tourist. I ask one of them to teach me the only Spanish song I want to know: "Guantanamera."

Yo soy un hombre sincero
De donde crece la palma
Y antes de morirme
Quiero echar mis versos del alma.

I am a sincere man
From where the palm tree grows
And before I die
I want to sing out the verses within my soul.

Afterwards, he hands me his card: Ernesto Velázquez Serrano, *Músico.*

Ernesto has one of the best jobs of all, and I tell him so. He can play his guitar for a few hours a day and earn a month's pay doing something he knows and loves. That is more than I've achieved in my whole life. He reflects on this and concedes that it is true. I offer to pay him 25 pesos as an artist's contribution for using his guitar.

"*¡No, no, muchacha!*" He shakes his head in amused embarrassment.

He points out his house, a green spot in the center of the outlying areas. I look at his card. Reparto Alcides Pino is the name of his *barrio* (neighborhood).

We walk to a nearby restaurant that looks impressive with a huge grass *palapa,* or thatched roof, and decoration throughout in tropical style, complete with giant wooden parrots. But this is not a tourist resort; this is a local eatery as evidenced by what eventually comes through the swinging doors. The pizza is the same pizza that can be bought from food carts for 5 pesos, a spongy white disk with a smear of something red and stringy yellow. My spaghetti is worse than the mush from a can. Yet the setting is spectacular, and the waiters are starched up and attentive.

Ernesto explains how his wife ran off with another man and how he has raised his three kids alone. "Nothing new here," I think to myself. He smiles at me gently.

"So, when will you come back to La Loma?" asks Ernesto Velázquez Serrano, *Músico.*

"I don't know . . . maybe tomorrow," I half-lie.

• • • •

I think of Charlotte, the stylish Danish woman I'd met standing in the visa-renewal queue in Havana. I remember the mistiness in her eyes as she spoke of her Cuban lover and dance teacher, of her plans to chuck her job as editor of the lifestyle section of a top Copenhagen newspaper, sell her three-bedroom Copenhagen condo, and begin a new, simple life with her soul mate in Havana.

I look at Ernesto and think, "If I see him the way he is probably seeing me, I could do a Charlotte." It strikes me that moments like these abound. At every turn there is always an opportunity to say yes or no. To smile or stare straight ahead. To connect or pass by barely rubbing shoulders. One day we may wake up and wonder why we said no way, José, why we stared straight ahead, why we passed up the chance for love, or even like.

Why indeed? Because it seemed like the right idea at the time.

16

THE LAST RESORT

Three pairs of eyebrows arch when I cheerfully recount my five hours of crooning on top of a hill with a Don Juan from "the shady side of La Loma." Three pairs of lips admonish me: "*Violencia . . . armas . . . mala gente . . . drogas . . . problemas . . .*"

I wonder if Juan Carlos and his family have ever ascended the 430 steps to the top of La Loma, the biggest hill in town, to gaze down at the poorer half of the city. They live in the sun; Don Juan lives in the shade. However, all eyebrows and lips relax a little when I play my halting version of "Guantanamera."

Yame goes upstairs complaining of a headache, and Juan asks me if I have any aspirin. Fortunately, I had packed a handful of Panadol Forte, the second most welcome gift in Cuba.

I take my offer of relief up to their room and find Yame propped against the wall, her head cradled in the crook of Juan's shoulder. With one hand he strokes her forehead and with the other her massive pregnant belly. Their marital bed is a stack of old mattresses and a tangle of crumpled sheets. An open window curtained with a worn towel looks down onto the broken concrete courtyard. I sit on a stool and watch them from a respectful distance, a pair of babes in the wood, clinging to each other for dear life.

The room is spare. In a society where freedom to aspire and be monetarily rewarded is limited, it seems that to have a child remains the most free-thinking, creative, and individualistic thing a couple can do. A reason for being.

● ● ● ●

After a few more days of waking on a plastic stretcher with my head half in the oven, I decide to visit Playa Blanca, a beach resort recommended by two German backpackers I met on the Sierra Maestra coast road. The resort is just north of Holguín on a flat road toward Guardalavaca, the big fat tourism sapphire of Oriente Province. In Guardalavaca rooms run to $150 per night, while barely around the next headland at Playa Blanca prices and star ratings drop to $5.00 a night and a black hole, respectively. I load up the bike with all my belongings in case I am not coming back, though I feel certain I will.

I start pedaling north. About a half an hour down the whisper-smooth *carretera* (highway), a bicycle draws even with me, then whips past. It is already a receding Lycra dot in the distance before I register that it was a touring cyclist with fancy waterproof panniers front and rear, which scream "foreigner." He did not even pause to say hello. Odd.

Sometime later, clearly having stopped to fix a flat or to relieve himself in some hidden location, the cyclist comes up from behind, but this time, he does slow down so that we can survey each other's kit. We ride along and quiz each other. Axel is a German on his first ever cycle tour. He purchased his shiny mountain bike for Christmas just a month ago. I figure that because he shot by without saying hello, he must be suffering from beginner cycle tourer's paranoia—the "Am I Going to Get There in Time?" syndrome—but I cannot be sure since he speaks no English and only rudimentary Spanish. I work out that he's visited Cuba five times, and each time he stayed in five-star Guardalavaca hotel rooms. After ten minutes he decides to tag along to my zero-star destination, which is mentally one crank turn for me, one giant *häschenhopfen* for Axel.

As we crest the rise, Playa Blanca appears with appealing blue cabins fronting the gentle arc of a quiet beach.

For $5.00 each we are shown to the prime cabin reserved exclusively for foreigners, which is a small rustic house with air-conditioning and color television. One drawback is its proximity to another of those confounded generators that chatter twenty-four hours a day to power the frosted lamps and gold-tapped showers of *las turistas* around the corner.

Axel and I are enamored by the little blue cabins, which rent for 12 pesos (60 cents) a night if you are Cuban and $5.00 otherwise. We look at each other and decide that neither of us passes for Castro's second cousin, so $5.00 it is. Each cabin sleeps six people on dubious-looking bunks and walls perforated with large mosquito-welcoming holes. The bathroom is a revival of the banana-rat hotel in Media Luna—that is, a concrete pit with a seatless toilet and a single cut-off pipe that delivers a solid stream of cold water to the chest.

I have lived and traveled for almost a year in Central America, and I've come to accept a less than puffy standard of pillow, but I fear for Axel, who is fresh from the land of precision engineering and *Vorsprung durch Technik* and who has experienced Cuba only from behind sealed tinted windows and sunken pool bars. I am not his *mutter,* however, and I think nothing further of it.

We trot across the hot sand to the resort restaurant for a meal. We are the only guests, save for a foursome of rowdy teenagers in the end cabin who brought a carload of their own food and a ghetto blaster. We get the outside table and the attention of both Jorge and David, who double as our waiters when not running about being receptionists, plumbers, hotel administrators, and potato peelers. The meal turns out to be very good: rice and beans, fried plantain, and fish for around $8.00. I mention that the price seems a little out of line with the standard of accommodations, a point eagerly noted by David, who is charged with the management and profitability of the resort. Even the smallest suggestions are carefully noted and considered, such as putting a molehill rather than a mountain of plantains on the plate to save money and still offer value.

Axel is upset that his meal arrives less than steaming hot, which is not surprising given the convoluted path from the stove through a gigantic concrete kitchen. The cook left early and Jorge had to reheat the food, perhaps with a cigarette lighter, we joke. As we eat a man with a guitar joins us and gleefully accepts a beer or three on Axel's account.

"*Jinetero,*" hiss Jorge and David disapprovingly. The word is used to describe, literally, "he who rides on the back of others," a hustler. It's not a respected profession at this end of the country either, but it must be worth it because more and more Cubans are doing it.

I take out my harmonica, and that is the last I see of it. I sincerely hope it is providing a living for someone.

Axel announces that he is disgusted by the bathroom in his cabin, stained and smelly due to a paucity of detergent and an abundance of cockroaches and lizards. But the final straw comes the next morning when he shoots out of his cabin, white and shaking and cursing the *ratten* and *rattensheiss* in his bed.

"NEVER! . . . AGAIN! . . . HERE!" he splutters hysterically.

"We are learning," says David quietly, now assuming the role of complaints manager.

For thirty years this resort has been a holiday center for 7,000 Cuban *trabajadores,* or ordinary workers. The 7,000 are rotated in shifts throughout the summer: June, July, and August. During this period the beach gets so full that it is known as Playa Perdóneme (Excuse Me Beach), as people clash shoulders in the water, trying to pass and be polite at the same time. It also seems a most accepting refuge for secluded international relations— that is, the amorous liaison *peligrosa* between foreigners and Cubans.

I meet a couple of Cuban girls languishing in the arms of their paunchy, balding Italian *novios.*

The two couples wander over to my patch of sand as I doodle in my diary. After the usual icebreakers, I ask the older girl, who makes me feel pale and dowdy, if she is going to get married.

"Yes, soon," she replies, baring a full set of white teeth and swinging her shock of raven hair over a spaghetti-strapped shoulder. "Wolfgang is going with me to Italy in July."

I note the order of names in that sentence and let her write her Holguín address in my diary, although I have not asked for it. Meanwhile, the males stay quiet and sheepish.

"*Jineteras,*" hisses Jorge for the second time, when I share my observations later.

Katalina, a name as romantic as her intent, tells me that the foursome is staying in a *casa particular* where the owners clearly turn a blind eye to Cuban–foreigner shenanigans, viewed by many as prostitution and viewed by me as a mixture of opportunism with a dash of good old-fashioned love. Some distance away, under the shade of a low-lying tree, a bespectacled Canadian woman with startled hair is getting entangled with a black Cuban *chico* with wandering hands and not caring who knows it.

Back at the cabins, Axel is demanding the return of his second $5.00 bill since we both paid for two days in advance. David pales; he's already submitted the accounts to the head office, so a refund is impossible.

A look of anxiety cum resignation crosses the countenance of the tall, wily German.

Five dollars spent is a night's accommodation wasted if he moves on now.

When the time comes next day for him to leave he disappears without so much as an *auf Wiedersehen,* let alone an e-mail address. Somehow he's lumped me, rat, and resort together. And I feel guilty.

I promise Jorge and David that I will send them an English–Spanish dictionary instead of a gratuity. For now, it is time to head back to Holguín.

• • • •

Back at the house of Juan Carlos, I carefully pack up for the nth time. It is now a formula: six bread rolls, three of which are stuffed with banana and jam and pressed into my circular lunch box, all water bottles fully charged, my washed knickers drying in a nylon string bag off the back of the bike. On this day Juan Carlos starts work again in the Guardalavaca resort and runs to join his coworkers on the *colectivo* bus that wheezes up the highway, looking forward to the generous gratuities that will insure him against the next cooking-oil drought. Dulce María and Yame wave me off, telling me to look for the *amarillos* (men in yellow jackets) who organize rides on passing trucks.

My intention is to pedal out of town and hitch a ride at least partway to the university town of Camagüey, 250 kilometers west. I know nothing of this place except the guidebook blurb about it being a "nice town," littered with giant-mouthed earthenware urns jauntily tilted in people's front yards to cool the rainwater that collects inside.

From there I will do a mixture of riding and hitching to the larger city of Santa Clara, where I have an address of a female friend of José de Santiago, perhaps the lover for whom he left Lolita. I stop at the outskirts where a man in a yellow jacket is busy organizing 10- to 15-peso (50- to 75-cent) rides to Havana on passing state trucks.

For such a random-looking operation, they have an impressive system going. It has been the same for the past twenty years. The *amarillo* knows which trucks will turn up when, if they are express or indirect, and all their stops. An urban transport system without rules, tickets, fancy shelters, or bus bays.

Havana is at least twelve hours away, and the wait for such a ride turns out to be a long one. I park my bike against a concrete wall and sit with the waiting locals, trying not to meet their sidelong glances, a reaction I recognize in myself as traveler fatigue.

I pass the time by watching three small burlap sacks twisting about on the dusty pavement. Now and then a fleshy pink snout perforated by two slimy slots thrusts through the holes in the corners, snuffling and snorting. I think of a squeeze bag of pork-flavored mustard. I wonder if the writhing sacks are any more aware of their destiny than I am of mine. Nearby, a pair of young goats waits patiently to board this landlocked Noah's ark.

Time passes, trucks pass. I am tempted to leap to my feet and climb aboard several trucks heading partway to Havana, but a curious lethargy keeps me rooted to the cement block in the shade. As the half hours pass, I find myself calculating how far I would get if I started pedaling instead of waiting, and I always come up with this answer: "Not far enough."

Finally, after we have been waiting for four hours, a giant, shallow tray truck creaks to a halt in front of us. There is a sudden flurry, a shouting and scampering to climb aboard with the *amarillos* struggling to collect the fare from each person. My bike and I are hoisted onto the back by a succession of strange hands, one pair opportunistically clamping across my breasts. People are packing themselves expertly into the tray like apples in a crate, and I wedge myself against a rice sack for some kind of protection against the inevitable jolts of monstrous potholes. I pull my bike and panniers close to me, feeling guilty about the space they are taking, but no one seems particularly bothered. Some wrap their heads entirely in a scarf or blanket and settle down for a nap. Others eat and drink and chat merrily.

As we wait for departure time, a young black *muchacho* slips into the space near my handlebars and proceeds to make small talk. He asks point blank if I will give him some money for dinner. He shows me his debit card and says that the money is in his account, but he simply forgot to take it out. I decline.

"No problem," he shrugs and smiles disarmingly, letting his long-lashed eyes slither down the sensuous curves of my bicycle. An alarm bell pings, and it isn't the one on my bike.

The first part of the trip is bearably smooth. The truck hurtles along like a comet in an asteroid belt, swerving to avoid potholes but at times joyfully diving for them like a duck into a puddle. Now and then the tray lifts and drops with a bone-shaking *crack!*

Nehehehehh says the little goat.

I shout, clamp my hands on my bike, and push myself farther into my rice sack. The wooden slats of the tray floor are disturbingly gap-toothed, and the slits are a little wider than I feel cozy with. Through the gaps I watch the raging torrent of road in close-up. I notice the left pedal of my bike poking through one of the gaps and spinning furiously in the undertow.

We drive through villages, slowing to respect the milling crowds that flock around the truck and climb aboard. At every small intersection the truck is besieged by sellers holding up poles laden with bags of coconut juice, fluorescent-colored rice-milk drinks, packets of extruded snacks, shelled peanuts, deep-fried disks of something sweet and sticky. No sooner have pesos and snacks passed in the air than the truck lurches forward, leaving the sellers flapping and stumbling alongside, trying to effect one last transaction.

The young *muchacho* opposite me introduces himself as Alfonso and strikes up conversation anew. I tell him I have not yet paid for the trip and he laughs, congratulating my good fortune. I tell him that I am going to stop in Camagüey. He thinks for a moment and shakes his head.

"Go all the way to Havana," he advises. "It is difficult to get an express truck like this; you ought to stay in the truck."

For the first time I am bumped off guard. My golden rule is to arrive at my destination with enough daylight to pitch the tent and light the stove, or, if traveling upscale, to find a free or cheap bed and locate a supermarket. This would be the case if I stick to my original idea of going to Camagüey.

Camagüey comes, Camagüey goes.

Somehow I have let this kid convince me that I should stay on the truck. "Never mind," I think. We'll be there soon, and I already have an address in Havana—that of the sister-in-law of Zaida from Manzanillo. I'll get a taxi if necessary, straight from the truck stop to their door. My bicycle folds up; there'll be no problem.

I settle into my rice sack.

• • • •

The sun sinks, and the relentless wind slowly changes from a warm heady breeze into a chilly headachy breeze, then to a cold, buffeting blast like a giant turbo fan in a refrigeration plant. I can see people rolling up into themselves, trying to get small enough to disappear into the dark recesses of the truck, tying their heads in plastic bags, quite unconcerned about suffocating in the quest to block the freezing wind.

I keep reaching into my pannier and pulling out clothing until there are no more layers to be layered. I feel sure that we are headed for Antarctica, not Havana. The woman and child to my right are shivering in the arms of her shirt-sleeved husband, and he has wrapped himself around his precious bundle as best he can. I lean across and pull the ground sheet from my tent and offer it to the bundle. They thank me in the darkness, proclaiming me a *persona buena* (good person). I take the large, stiff plastic bag from around my tent and put my head and shoulders inside. This proves effective for an hour, until a huge gust snatches it from my hands. I watch it dance away like a bat on speed into the night sky.

Nehehehehh.

Several people are now swigging rum from small bottles to numb their nerve endings. They are becoming more and more boisterous with each burning gulp. We are somewhere out in the country now, but the absence of moon or stars gives the impression of hurtling through deep space.

A pair of dim lights suddenly appears on the horizon. As they draw closer I think of a giant black panther opening its eyes wider and wider until we are staring into its retinas. The yellow-eyed animal leaps forward, then off to one side . . .

KRAAAANNNNNNNGG!

Nehehehehh.

The truck weaves slightly; sparks fly; a woman screams. Someone is shouting. The truck slows suddenly, then stops. We all lurch forward and then back into our rice sacks and dirty tires. The sudden lack of wind is a relief. Cigarette lighters flame up like little candles.

I pull out my flashlight and see the damage: a big yellow bus has clipped the truck, as well as a couple of people who unfortunately had limbs protruding. The damage is, however, slight. One woman, sobbing hysterically, has a deep gash in her arm. Someone says something about a *doctora* being in the back of the truck, but she has no supplies. I scramble over with the only useful things I have on hand, a vial of antiseptic powder and a small sticking plaster. I sprinkle the powder on the cut, explaining what it is. The woman is clearly in shock, screaming at her spouse and the world in general. Another man's pate has been sliced, but he seems all right. With the woman still sobbing and cursing, I crawl back to my rice sack with people around me saying *"persona buena."* We sit there in the darkness, and I notice the intensity of the Milky Way for the first time since getting on the truck.

After about half an hour of waiting, the engine starts. The woman has calmed down now. Life shifts into first gear.

Around 8:00 P.M. the truck pulls into a small town where passengers can get a bite to eat. I hesitate about leaving my things on the truck, but I need to find a toilet. I use "foreigner power" and approach some people sitting on rocking chairs on a tiny porch in front of a decrepit old house. They say nothing but nod toward the door, rocking, rocking. I enter their world briefly, walking through their bedroom to a tiny bathroom with, surprisingly, a flush toilet. I leave them a peso.

Back outside some Cubans, the richer ones, are eating plates of food from street stalls; the majority purchase a snack from the vendors swarming around the truck. I climb back into the truck and rummage for one of the three packets of cookies I bought for the journey, intending to share them. I have been beaten to it.

The cookies are gone, as are the six bread rolls I had packed. I ask around. I am met by a circle of innocence. One man shakes his head. *"Sin vergüenza,"* he admonishes those present. The thieves are without shame.

I notice that Alfonso has vanished. I think of my disinclination to buy him dinner earlier and stop my mind from going further. One of the men in the truck points to my bike, specifically to the left crank. The left pedal is gone, probably snatched by the wind and constant vibration. Yes, this one looks more like the work of the gods than do the purloined cookies.

"You can get a replacement at any *ponchero*" (puncture repairer), the man says helpfully. "If you want to come to Havana, I will take you to my friend's place."

On checking the bike more closely, I notice that some deft fingers have unzipped my tool bag and made off with my Ritchey CoolTool and puncture repair kit. Probably while I was playing doctor to the hysterical woman.

The CoolTool, an object of some desire, was a farewell gift from a friend when I left Australia four years ago, though in all honesty I have never used it. I suspect that the new owner will establish a bicycle repair shop with this single gadget; such is the resourcefulness of the Cuban people. There is still no sign of Alfonso, and there isn't going to be.

I think of all the times I have tried to save money in my world travels, or was less than forthcoming in my generosity, or even committed an act of dishonesty in the misguided attempt to get ahead (for example, not returning excess change from a purchase).

Each and every time I have paid for my action, usually ten to twenty times over. The CoolTool was worth around $20, and a single meal for Alfonso would have been around 50 cents. The truck trip, which I have not paid for, would have been a couple of dollars. In Costa Rica I once bargained with a taxi driver to reduce his fare for a certain trip from $20 to $12 and subsequently left my bag—containing a good headband, my keys, a Mini Maglite, and a small Swiss army knife—in the car. The worst thing is that I never seem to learn. All I do is continue to commit acts of stinginess to reinforce my common mortal fear that I will never have enough money and will thus die a bag lady in some nameless, stinking gutter.

• • • •

The truck moves off, and I settle into my rice sack. I am beat. My brain is also working overtime as to how I might get my bike back into pedaling order. We enter deep space again, and I huddle down behind my panniers and face the dirty bottom of the truck to stay out of the wind as much as possible. I tell all and sundry to let me know when the Santa Clara turnoff approaches. My fellow travelers do more than that: Around 11:00 P.M. they whistle and shout and bang on the roof of the cabin to signal that someone wants to get off. To my horror the truck does not stop. My cohorts simply shrug. Perhaps this really is a *directo* with a stickler for rules at the wheel.

By this time I feel like a bag of frozen peas pulled from the freezer and slapped on a kitchen bench a few times. I weakly ask how much further to Havana.

"*Tres horas*" is the reply.

Three hours!

I decide that I cannot survive that long and prepare to meet my icy death. I spend the next half hour embalming myself in my tent fly. About an hour and a half later, the truck pulls into a fluorescent-lit twenty-four-hour cafe in the middle of nowhere. This place is known as Aguada de Pasajeros, or "watering hole for passengers." The curious thing is how cold and damp it is, more reminiscent of misty Ireland than Cuba.

Not wanting to pass another second in that freezing vortex, I get the hell off that truck with the help of a mildly inebriated young man, because by now all remaining delegates and delinquents are well and truly plastered on rum.

I count my panniers and tent: one, two, three . . . and roll my bike into the cafe. I sit down at a table to thaw out, collect my thoughts, and ruminate over my unrideable bicycle. It is 2:00 A.M. The sandwich bar is still open, with nothing on display. I explain myself to the large woman spilling over the counter, asking if I can hang out at the cafe until morning. She leads me around the back of her kitchenette so that I can sit beside the giant urn of steaming coffee, which I hug as gratefully as a lover and do not let go. I watch as she dispenses 20-centavo (about 1 cent) coffees to the dribble of walk-ins as she has done every day for the past twelve years. I watch as she chats with each and every stranger as if she knows them like a brother, which she basically does.

"Aside from the occasional foreigner, I know every truck, and every person that comes here, and the approximate time they will turn up, and what they will be drinking, and how sweet," she claims.

I gratefully accept a ham and cheese toasted *bocadito* despite my resolve never to eat anything of the sort ever again in Cuba.

I fall asleep in the plastic chair with the airline blanket I stole draped over my head. I will worry about *mañana . . . mañana.*

17

THE RICHEST HOUSE IN CUBA

I manage to fall unconscious with the coffee urn in my arms, and despite everything I have suffered in the preceding twelve hours, I do not dream about the truck ride from hell.

I open one eye to see a shaft of the new day finger its way across the floor to where I am slumped in my chair. The trickle of *pasajeros* desperately seeking their daily caffeine jolt has become a steady stream as the sky slowly lightens.

I heave myself out of the plastic chair I had made my bed for the night, thank my hosts, and wheel my one-pedaled bike outside for a better look at the damage. One of the gear shifters spins freely on the handlebar, seemingly broken. I curse myself for chattering during that bicycle maintenance course I took four years ago, and I set about blindly unscrewing and prodding and poking whatever looks unscrewable, proddable, and pokeable. I thank my lucky stars the new owner of my CoolTool did not take my uncool multiwrench as well.

After I cobble the mechanism back together, it miraculously works. A spring must have come unsprung in the twelve hours of bumping and grinding in the back of the truck. Now, with just the left pedal missing, the bike is merely half-rideable. I hail every truck, car, and combine harvester that enters the parking lot for a ride to Santa Clara, about 60 kilometers east, but most people are heading to Havana or to a nearby village. One very friendly foursome offers me a lift back to Havana, advising me that there are better bike shops there. But as a stubborn cyclist hell-bent on completing her route, I am not ready to admit defeat and return to Havana just yet.

I wheel the bike onto the highway and try waving a dollar bill at the passing traffic, which amounts to one vehicle every ten minutes. I switch to a $5 bill, but still no one stops. One pickup truck with a private license plate does stop and asks for $10; when I show him $5, he refuses and roars off with an empty tray. Money changes everything, and money is changing the heart of Cuba.

Finally, I wheel the bike back to the parking lot. A group of four workers in a vehicle with blue license plates, signifying that it is state-owned, offers me a ride to Sancti Spíritus, a town only 83 kilometers south of Santa Clara. Alternatively, they offer to dump me at the Santa Clara turnoff. Faced with being stranded with a nonfunctional bicycle on a quiet Sunday in the baking heat, I hesitate. I had my heart set on Santa Clara, and to change now feels like waiting in the gate lounge for a flight to Africa and being asked if I'd mind going to Sweden instead. People get attached to their itineraries, and I am repeatedly disturbed to discover that I am no different. I was drawn to Santa Clara because of an address scratched on a piece of paper. A promise of a place to stay with someone I do not know but who, because of a vague connection, might roll out the welcome mat. Somewhere to park my weathered tires, to lay my weary head, to return to the womb. No matter how free we think we are, we are creatures of contact. We seek security in every decision. Why not Sancti Spíritus? Hey, it starts with the same letter as Santa Clara.

I accept the ride.

I squeeze between Roberto and his brother, Mauricio, in the front seat, while their two coworkers share the back, and we head down the highway on which I'd nearly frozen to death just hours before. In daylight it is now a cheerfully sunny *camino* to cheerful, sunny Sancti Spíritus. We stop at a high-tech highway gas station, air-conditioned to meat-fridge temperatures, where I am able to buy, at a U.S. price, a battery for my camera. I feel self-conscious about spending close to $10 on this purchase with Roberto hovering in the background. That's half a doctor's monthly wage in Cuba. Twice Lolita's wage.

• • • •

In the absence of a decent breakfast, I buy a dollar packet of sugar cookies shaped like teddy bears. It's a sickly way to start the day, but I'm desperate. We approach the Santa Clara turnoff. Roberto turns to me, indicating my option to jump out and wait for another ride. Secure in the care of my newfound friends, however fleeting, I decide to stay in the car.

We talk. Roberto lives in Havana with his brother and their wives and children. They are on their way to Sancti Spíritus to do some "paperwork" at a hospital, which will take about an hour or two. Then it is back to Havana. The two coworkers in the back are clearly along for the ride, perhaps a Sunday out with the boys, a chance to play hooky away from their families and their unvarying routine, at the state's expense.

• • • •

We arrive in Sancti Spíritus within two hours. Roberto decides that first, we will go to a *ponchero* to get a pedal for my bike. We drive down a back lane to a small house. He instructs me to stay in the car, saying that the mere glimpse of a foreigner is likely to triple the price.

"They'll charge you $10 or more!" he exclaims.

The men disappear around the back of the house with my bike. After a few minutes they emerge, and grafted to the left crank is an old tattered plastic pedal that the *ponchero* had removed from his personal Huffy. The cost? Four dollars, or 80 pesos. The price is absurd, and I'll never know if it was the *ponchero* or my rescuers who extracted a handsome margin. Later, when I recounted the tale of the purloined pedal, many Cubans shook their heads, saying that such a pedal would have cost no more than 30 pesos, or $1.50, brand new and that I had been royally gypped.

"*Sin vergüenza!*" they exclaimed, insisting that only those who were "without shame" would go so low as to misrepresent a price to anyone, foreigner or otherwise.

I decide that the real bottom line is that my problem is solved. I pay Roberto the $4.00, plus a $2.00 tip. To his credit he excitedly tells me to stop as I go to count out more bills.

Roberto lets me off at the first *casa particular* that has a sign hanging out front offering rooms. He gives me his address in Havana and invites me to stay with his family when I get back. I say sure. But I think, "Maybe not, you opportunistic bastard."

Of course, I can now look at the paltry sum of $4.00 and think, "What on earth was I hung up about?"

I was rescued, I was transported, I was helped. They are poor, I am rich. They had a rare chance to make a few windfall dollars for their families, and they took it. Yet I somehow got indignant over the luxury item called principle. Perhaps because I fancied that I was one of them, living and breathing and scraping by like a Cuban, adopting their daily problems and concerns (albeit somewhat selectively), in this instance the concern of paying too much for something.

Still in my presumptuously local yokel mode, I knock at the door of the *casa,* Los Espejos. It is clearly the most affluent *casa particular* I have laid eyes on to date. Inside, you could be standing in any middle-class comfortable First World home. The kitchen is sleek, with decorative tiles punctuating the white ones every third tile, and the countertop features an impressive lineup of electrical appliances: blender, microwave, deep fryer, food processor, and one I cannot identify that has Braun embossed on it.

The owner, a large woman with immaculate red nails, greets me with a fat, wet lipsticked smile as she pops great joints of chicken into a plug-in appliance that goes *psssshhhhhhh* when she closes the lid and presses one of the blinking buttons. The familiar Cuban cookware, a large blackened tin pot dented from being swooshed over coals, is nowhere to be seen.

• • • •

The hostess rents out five guest rooms upstairs and runs a private little *paladar* (private restaurant) downstairs, which is actually the family living room. The tables are intimately set with lace cloths, fine glassware, cozy chairs, and candles. The walls are all but obscured by tooled brass decorations. A giant stereo system dominates the bar, and the light from crystal and gold lamps bathes the numerous objets d'art poised on polished furniture. On this day a party of six Italian tourists are tucking into lobster.

Four of the five guest rooms, which rent for $25 per night, are already occupied, as they are for most of the year, the owners tell me. I calculate that they must be taking in at least $200 to $300 a day. I negotiate $15 a night, including breakfast and dinner, stressing that I want nothing more fancy than rice and beans and salad with perhaps some fried plantain. They agree, but from that point on the service I receive suggests loud and clear I am cargo class.

I am so hungry that I agree to a fried-chicken lunch even before changing my attire or unloading my bike. I am seated at a table on my own. The six Italians are now into the coffee, tiramisu, and ebullient conversation. I nod to the occupants of another table in the corner, a Cuban *muchacha* nudging twenty years old (I note the pair of ripe cantaloupes fighting to escape from her tight black top) and, sitting opposite, her fawning, graying *esposo de Italia,* a fifty-something gent hunched over a glass of wine. Their body language is intriguing: She speaks and gestures with an air of confidence, teeth gleaming, eyes alive with material contentment. He, on the other hand, looks like a man who is getting laid on the sly but doesn't want anyone to find out. He seems to shrink before my eyes, almost disappearing through the seat of his chair.

"We spend half the year in Cuba, half the year in Italy," she says, her voice tinkling like a small wind chime. She casts a loving look across at Romeo. He smiles sheepishly and shrinks even smaller until there is a tiny figure twitching and shuffling about in the middle of the seat. I give the poor man a break and turn back to my meal.

As I eat, the members of the family swan in and out of the room, seemingly multiplying with each reappearance. They glide across the floor, the new economic royalty cloaked in designer jeans, makeup, gold watches, large rings, and gold pendants. One by one they fire the same questions at me about my trip but curiously don't wait for a response. Outside, a nephew is tossing strips of lobster to one of the several pedigree dogs lolling in the driveway.

The food does look good. I take another bite of my chicken and a sip of the juice. It takes me a few bites to realize that something is missing. Flavor? I think of $5.00-a-month Lolita in Santiago de Cuba, her oily little camping stove, the wonderful flavors that came from it, her dressing table adorned with empty shampoo bottles, the sprig of thyme growing in her rusty tin can on the fence. Something is missing from the food here. I think it is love.

I go upstairs and survey the room. Well-appointed and comfortable. I close the door and lie down on the bed, thankful for the luxury that my money can buy when I allow myself to let go of it. There is a knock at the door. Before I can answer, it opens and two of the younger members of the family tumble in. They bounce on the bed beside me. A third carries a basket of laundry through my room to the second door, which leads to the roof and the upstairs clothesline, asking permission but not waiting for the OK. They fire more questions, rolling about on the bed in new jeans without holes, fancy belt buckles, and manicured fingernails. I suddenly feel that I am no longer in Cuba.

Then again, I notice that even the poorest Cuban women keep their nails manicured and their hair perfect. Here, the mating ritual is still something to fuss over, not just a brief release forced into the space between hitting the alarm buzzer, hitting the office, hitting the remote control, hitting the kids, then hitting the hay. In America sex therapists almost outnumber television sets. I haven't come across any in Cuba.

The nine-year-old, a confident poppet dressed like an eighteen-year-old, asks me if I'd like a *pluma*, a ballpoint pen. I don't hear correctly and mumble something about already having given all my pens away. She shakes her finger and opens the cupboard to reveal a large box of about a hundred brand-new pens. She insists that I take one. This is the first time I am offered a pen by a "poor local," rather than the other way around. The moment looms large. The collage of impressions I have collected since entering this house—the offhand service, bland food, trappings of excess, lobster-eating dogs, and, to cap it off, the freely offered ballpoint pen—seem to coalesce into one coherent howl from the lips of every member of this family: *I never want to be poor again.*

In the evening I ask for rice and beans and salad and wait an eternity while another group of foreigners enjoys the lobster and tiramisu. My beans arrive cold, and I ask to have them warmed slightly. I wait an eternity for them to arrive; indeed, the husband of the house starts to clear my dishes away before I make him aware that I was just starting my meal. He notes my Oakley sunglasses and asks if he can buy them from me. I tell him they cost me $80, and he offers to pay $50. I tell him I need them to ride my bike.

• • • •

I decide to take my newly old left pedal out for a sunset spin. Sancti Spíritus is a curiously tranquil town that lives up to its spiritual sounding name: Narrow flagstone streets fan out from the town square like a spider web, and an imposing powder-blue church watches silent and stoic over an eighteenth-century stone bridge built by the Spanish.

While I plod back up the hill toward the guest house, a *chico* draws level with me and asks questions in very good English about my life in general. He is employed as a guide for a tour company and loves to speak English. He invites me to a singing concert in town that evening. After quizzing him further, I work out that it is karaoke, a new form of entertainment in Cuba and quite a hit.

His friend Yobani lives in a very modest stone house with his parents around the corner from Los Espejos. They sit me down and offer me coffee, watching me intently as I sip and talk. Yobani's father, a huge man who taxes the limits of his woven plastic chair, heaves himself up to hug me and invites me to try his signature dessert, flan. It is warm, just out of the oven, and very comforting. I instantly notice the modest and welcoming atmosphere in this simple home. They invite me to stay. I wish I had met them earlier that day, before encountering Los Espejos.

Yobani makes an income carving animals from wood and selling them to hotels and restaurants. The family presents me with a beautiful dolphin he has carved from ceiba. I hesitate, my mind calculating the available space in my panniers and the fragility of this object of beauty.

I have made the transition from a stuff-filled life (house, car, furniture, washer and dryer, microwave oven, objets d'art, and enough shoes to make Imelda Marcos feel like a barefoot monkess) to a stripped-down traveling life (folding bicycle, two panniers, and a tent). I feel that my new simplified life makes it impossible to carry anything that is not multifunctional or fundamental to my existence.

This wooden dolphin means the world to me in this moment, holding it in both hands with Yobani and his parents looking on, the slightly burnt, milky smell of caramel flan hovering in the air, the squeak of the plastic webbing straining under the weight of Yobani's father. If I take it with me, the context fades; it becomes just another dust collector sitting on the shelf of an air-conditioned, carpeted, dishwasher-equipped house. I hope not, but who knows what the future holds? I do not want to take the risk.

I make a decision. I gently explain that I am at a point of simplifying my life, that their giving me the gift in their home is the gift, and that I do not need to possess it. I think they understand. I accept the gift. And then I give it back to them, returning it to the world where it belongs.

18

LONG ENOUGH IN TRINIDAD

Per cubic meter, the "museum town" of Trinidad is probably the most hyped, the most moneyed, and the most back-packed in all of Cuba.

It's the must-see of the guidebook top five, the sidebar favorite of fawning high-season travel writers and a beneficiary of the wave of the UNESCO World Heritage wand. To go there is to succumb to the hype. To purposely avoid going there is also to succumb to the hype. I decide to succumb and see what the hype is all about.

The ride to Trinidad from Sancti Spíritus is a mere 70 kilometers, flat and easy. I even pause at a concrete bus shelter to chat for an hour or more with an Austrian couple riding their bikes in the opposite direction. We eat our trail mix, talk about life and love and waterproof panniers, compare the calorific contents of our lunch bags in detail, then part forever without exchanging e-mail addresses.

When I first started traveling, I felt compelled to stay in touch with every single person I paused with for more than five minutes, usually by offering my e-mail address. When they did not offer theirs in return, I was left pondering, and when they didn't respond to my e-mails, I felt royally dissed. Especially if they promised to write. It took me a long time to accept that a travel connection, like a battery, expires. That moment can be as far off as when one of you dies, or as immediate as the next intake of breath. The connection can be temporarily recharged with a flurry of e-mails, but over time, and without connecting face to face again, its magical power drains away.

Out of sight is out of mind. The Austrian couple was a diminishing dot on my mind's horizon by the time another couple came over the hill and stopped for a chat. A couple touring in the comfort of their coupledom with their mutually agreed upon schedules and petty arguments and compromises, their decisions about what $50 hotel to choose or what Fodor's-endorsed must-see they must see. In these moments an addiction to my lone travel quest borders on a kind of solo-traveler snobbery, which I recognize as little more than a cry for someone, anyone, to acknowledge that I exist.

About 6 kilometers outside of Trinidad itself, I spot a sign pointing to the Manaca Iznaga. A big star indicates that it is some kind of tourist attraction, so with time on my hands, I go for it. The road leads to an impressive and well-maintained *hacienda* with a tall tower on the grounds outside. The guidebook tells me that I am standing in the Valley of the Sugar Mills and looking at the house of Pedro Iznaga, a man who made a mint from slavery in 1795.

The tower was used to watch over and summon the slaves, who from so high up must have looked like plastic figurines on a giant green game board. All around the base of the tower vendors have strung up clotheslines with white lace tablecloths flapping in the breeze, like a giant Christo sculpture come untethered. I climb to the top of the tower, all 44 meters of it, pausing to take in the view though the large arched cut-outs on all four sides. From the top the fields roll out as far as the eye can see. I halfheartedly try to take a picture, but as I predict, the viewfinder presents me with a mundane postage-stamp image that could be a picture of anywhere. I lower my camera.

Admiring the view at the top is a Canadian woman who has paid a local *señora* $25 to be her personal guide for the day. I ask the guide to recommend an inexpensive place to stay in Trinidad.

"Everything is very expensive in Trinidad," she says, and offers a room in her house for $30. I blanch, and in that instant she sees that I am not her target market and goes back to attending to someone who is.

●●●●

As I continue on toward Trinidad, a car pulls alongside, and a business card is thrust into my face. "Rent room," says the occupant, and speeds off.

I notice that the *casa particular* stickers start right at the outskirts of Trinidad. There is a man tending a newly planted patch of grass out the front of one of them, and I stop to check what is on offer. It is a beautiful house, squeaky clean, with comfortable sofas and a television, and a bargain at $12 a night. The whole family comes out to campaign for my custom. They have only just gotten their license to legally operate. I tell them I'll think about it. Eight dollars, they offer. This is a great deal, and I feel guilty about wanting to go into the town to check other options. I feel like giving these people a break, being their first guest. I tell them that I'll be back if I do not find anything comparable.

"You do not like our house?" The *señora* looks at me, searchingly.

"It's beautiful," I say truthfully, feeling a strong pull to make their day. But I just need to see if there is something closer to the center.

I make my way into the first main square and am assailed by cries of "*Casa?*" from all directions, all shapes, all ages. The town, quaint and colonial, is predictably bursting with accommodation, yet I am looking for something that will take me to the heart of the people, not merely back to another $10-a-night room. I move on, in no particular direction, fending off the usual barrage of questions from groups of touts at every corner. On one corner I notice a tall man with a thick black moustache leaning against a window, drinking coffee. He is over thirty, so he has my attention.

"Are you looking for a room?" he asks.

"Is it your house, or your friend's house?" I ask.

"No, no, it is my house."

He downs the last drop of his coffee and beckons me to follow.

"How much?" I ask anxiously. I stop him from walking. "I only want to pay $10 a night, including simple food," I say.

He gently takes my bike from me and keeps walking. Normally, I would whip out my machete and sever his arms at the wrist for taking control of my Bike Friday, but there is something about this man that exudes integrity.

We walk together. "Are you sure it's your house?" I ask again, feeling somewhat silly.

He nods. "I have a license."

We arrive at a little white building sandwiched between two others and go upstairs. It is a simple apartment with two rooms.

One for Ivan, my escort, and his wife, Mirella, and one for his thirteen-year-old daughter—"*la niña,*" they call her. They want to give me their marital bed; Mirella will sleep with her daughter since *la niña* gets scared if she has to sleep alone, and Ivan will sleep at his mother's place down the road.

In the small, modest lounge room stands a giant remote-control Sony television, a gift from German friends who had passed through. *La niña,* bespectacled and big for her age, spends most of her time in deep conference with the set, says Ivan, despite the bland offerings on one or two channels.

For some reason I feel at home here. I had formulated a somewhat cynical opinion about licensed houses based on my experience in Sancti Spíritus, and now I have met a couple who will change that view, I hope.

• • • •

Ivan produces all the documentation to prove that his is a licensed house. In reality I am not bothered, although he does point out that the paperwork proves they are operating a business and are less likely to steal my stuff, as has happened to some tourists.

"They'll take you to their house, feed you, offer a cheap deal, and when you return from your day of sightseeing, everything will be gone—everything, including them," he says, echoing the words of Lolita in Santiago de Cuba.

He also shows me pictures of himself and his German pals, partying with his family in some exotic *extranjero* hangouts, drinking dollar wine, eating dollar food. Unfortunately, I am not one of those *extranjeros.*

I unload my bags and announce that I will cook dinner for

them in the evening, using pasta and tomato sauce from somewhere in my panniers and some Asian greens that I picked up from a market somewhere along the way.

I go back into town and walk Trinidad's famous cobbled streets.

I could be in Granada, Nicaragua, or Granada, Spain, although I have visited only the former and seen pictures of the latter. Museums line the central streets. Not being one for museums, I simply stay outside and soak up the atmosphere. I feel as if I am captive in colonial Toy Town.

Beyond the city center a path leads up the hill to a radio transmitter. The half-hour hike takes me almost an hour, for I am stopped by some Cuban women basking in the sun. They welcome me to join the group, but their intentions soon come clear. They want me to buy some of their wares, baskets and urns, which they produce from under their flowing dresses.

I hike on. At the top stands the 180-meter-high tower surrounded by wire fencing. Below lies the sweeping Valle de los Ingenios, the Valley of the Sugar Mills. I sit and admire the view. A man descends from the tower and offers to unlock the gate and let me enter the compound. Silvio, the lone watchtower man, does not take long to tell me his life story. He is divorced, naturally, and finds it lonely sitting on top of the hill. I point out that it seems like a tranquil, spiritual life, mindful, however, of what my good friend Kev Duggan once said: "Anything is great for not too long."

"When will you return?" asks Silvio.

"Soon," I say, without really thinking. I think back to Ernesto, the *trovador* on top of La Loma de la Cruz in Holguín who taught me "Guantanamera." "When will you return?" he had asked, with eyes searching mine. I am moving faster than these people, and I notice that their sincerity is as deep as mine is shallow.

I wander back down the hill and into town, where I am immediately accosted by a group of pushy women selling jewelry. They follow me, then poke me with their fingers when I try to walk away.

"No, thank you. No, thank you. I don't want it. No . . ." I lose my composure for a split second. "Fuck, Trinidad is horrible!" I suddenly blurt out. The woman who has planted her nose about an inch from mine yanks it back like I've spat in her eye and throws up her hands theatrically.

"Oh, my!" she exclaims with mock horror and daggerish sarcasm, then spins on her heel and stalks off.

••••

I pass by a watchmaker's nook. This is the front room of a house where a young *muchacho* is working at a small table set with an array of rusty-looking components. My prized Casio world time watch, bought from a sale bin in an Irish supermarket, is starting to fade away, and as it is the only watch I've found that displays a tiny map of the world with a moveable dateline, I am desperate to revive it. Sergio the watch repairer meticulously takes apart the casing and dips the parts into liquid, but nothing changes. In fact, the face goes blank, and that is the last time it tells any kind of time.

While he works I survey his world, laid out on the little table. There are several old watches in a neat row, some working, most not, dirty with broken bands. I could donate mine to his livelihood, for he can use it for parts. But I am too attached to my dying watch, which tells me the time in places I will probably never get to, places where 9:00 A.M. and 5:00 P.M. are as significant as any other hour on its scratched face. I have a hard time letting it go.

Sergio's mother emerges from the shadows and gives me the address of her other house in Sancti Spíritus, offering me lodging there if and when I next pass through. She beckons me to sit down in their best chair, a tattered old thing I am careful not to sit too far into, and offers me a coffee. I ask to use the bathroom and they apologize, for in between watch repairs Sergio is rebuilding the house, a place he has lived for all of his thirty-four years. The rest of the house behind the repair table is little more than a pile of dusty rubble and twisted cable, and somewhere in there is a broken, dirty bowl that I had hoped was connected to a drain of some sort. I give Sergio a dollar for trying to fix my watch.

Months later, I receive a beautiful letter from him. I know it is beautiful because my Costa Rican friend Carlos tells me so.

"I wish I could write a letter like that," he says, clearly emotional as he reads the crooked handwritten Spanish.

In the letter Sergio asks me to send some batteries for his watch business. Later I send mail to many friends in Cuba, but none of it arrives in their hands.

I arrive back at Ivan and Mirella's house to find a pot of pasta boiling on the stove and a can of tomatoes opened, bought from the dollar store. My packet of pasta and long-life tomato sauce sit unopened on the counter. Perhaps they thought I would ask for a price reduction if they used my ingredients. Perhaps they thought a guest should not have to provide ingredients in a *casa particular.* Perhaps they are simply kind, generous people.

I pull out some two-day-old bread rolls that are already in an advanced stage of rigor mortis and try prodding and poking them to life. Mirella takes one look and says *"Bótalo"* (toss it). I offer to fry the Asian greens with a little oil and garlic, and she looks on with a mixture of curiosity and mistrust. As we eat our pasta meal, I can see that the family is not accustomed to this type of foreigner food. It reminds me of my parents entertaining Caucasian guests back in Sydney, and the look on Mrs. Kneeshaw's face when she and her husband sat down to face a giant bowl of chicken feet soup prepared by my Shanghainese father.

I spend a couple more days in that house, cycling to Playa Ancón, a tourist cove a half- hour ride to the coast. An imposing, 1950s-style hotel commands the beach, which is dotted exclusively with pale bodies. I sit for a long time under the shadow of an anorexic palm tree, watching the stream of tourists avail themselves of the beachside bar.

In the evening I go walking in the cobbled streets with Ivan. Most places are closed. We find a semi-outdoor bar where a band is playing, and we stand outside the ring of topiary trees so as to listen without committing ourselves to an inflated foreigner cover charge. The doorman comes over and has words with Ivan.

"They are critical of us being together," he explains when the doorman backs off.

A Cuban socializing with a foreigner is often looked upon by his fellow countrymen as opportunistic, conniving, and generally acting above his station in life. Yet from what I observe, virtually every Cuban uses ingenuity and opportunity in some form simply to get by, and fraternizing with a foreigner is just one of those techniques. The Cuban people are proud, and I suspect it niggles them to watch a brother capitulate to "foreign aid."

We pop into various places where drink and music are on

offer. As I don't really drink, in that a single drink will last me all night, making me the world's cheapest date, we sit at several tables simply talking about life in Cuba and Ivan's hopes for the future of his daughter, ignoring the eyes boring into our backs.

The following night I ask for simple rice and beans and salad, the fare I have become quite content with on my trip to date. At the table I am presented with a large fish, grilled in oil and garlic and onions and smelling utterly delicious. The fish must have cost at least $3.00, a large sum of money. As we eat and make small talk, Ivan asks me how long I intend to stay. I tell him that I will leave tomorrow. He nods and goes quiet.

Sometime later he announces that he thinks it would be a very good idea for me to stay another day, to relax, see more of Trinidad. I tell him I'd love to, but no, I must move on.

"No, I really think you should stay another day," he says. Finally, Mirella says, "Please stay another day to help us."

• • • •

The truth is that Ivan and Mirella are finding it difficult to raise the funds for the monthly license fee. If they default, they will lose it. I am unable to respond and gently ask out of genuine curiosity why they bought such an expensive item, the fish, when they knew they would have trouble paying the dues.

It was a rhetorical question, and Ivan simply shrugs. It could well have been an act to encourage me to stay. But I am not going to stay another night, even though I now want to. I give them an extra $5.00.

I should give them more. I should stay another ten nights with these wonderful, hopeful people.

The next morning I pack up my bags and bid farewell to

Ivan and Mirella; *la niña* is still upstairs glued to the big screen. I flag down a passerby and ask him take a picture of us gathered around my bicycle. In my lunch box are four fresh bread rolls that Mirella scouted out for me early that morning.

"Write to us," Mirella says.

I leave Trinidad knowing little of its history, music, or museum collections and caring even less, but I am determined to return one day for no other reason than to see Ivan and Mirella again.

19

A LOITER TOO FAR

I am at a crossroads. I can tackle the near-vertical ascent to Topes de Collantes, a cool, foggy town of health resorts for vacationing Cuban bigwigs, then take a reportedly fantastic 20-kilometer descent down the mountain into Santa Clara, the town that has eluded me on two significant occasions. Or I can continue around the coast to Cienfuegos, which will probably be another tourist trap like Trinidad, given its proximity to Havana. Those holidaymakers on get-back-to-work-Monday beach packages in Varadero would normally venture no farther than Cienfuegos or Trinidad by air-conditioned bus, if at all.

I am drawn toward the mountain option, despite being warned that the road is extremely steep, particularly when encumbered with a three-month life-support system strapped to two skinny wheels. But after four years of traveling on a bicycle, I have learned that things take as long as they take. When I had a day job and a car and a jacket with padded shoulders, I thought a twenty-minute drive down the highway at an illegal speed was a raw inconvenience. Now, I allow all day to get wherever I have to get, no matter how near or far it is. Thus, I am prepared to spend an entire day pushing my bike uphill to Topes de Collantes.

On my way out of Trinidad, I spot a foreigner on a bicycle. It is an English gentleman who has recently retired, and he's left behind a somewhat alarmed family in the UK while he bikes around Cuba for a month. I give him the address of Ivan and Mirella in Trinidad, almost begging him to stay with them. It is the best thing I can do for my friends, short of giving them all my money. He rides off cheerily, promising to stay with them and to e-mail me with details of his journey. I give him my e-mail address in "passing lane" mode—that is, I do not ask for his. I never hear from him again.

I reach the turnoff to Topes de Collantes and boldly set off toward the hills. The sun has risen to near melting point despite the early hour of the day, and I am thankful for the shade cast by the steep sides of the mountains as the road starts to ascend. Just 2 kilometers up the mountain the gradient rises sharply and my little wheels stop dead. At this point I am in direct sunlight. I get off the bike and start pushing as planned, but I feel my feet sliding back down the hill, like the folk clinging to the deck in the movie *Titanic* as the ship goes vertical. Ironically, it's often easier to ride up a steep hill than push the bike; when pushing, the body is off to one side, so the force is not optimally centered.

Pant, pant.

My head is a giant stuffed pot roast in the heat. I flash back to the infuriating eleven or so rivers I crossed in northwest Scotland in 1997, straining hour after hour on the long, tedious ascents, barely recovering on the short, unsatisfying descent down to creek-bed level.

Pant, pant.

I flash back to the UK, where I pulled a fully loaded suitcase trailer to the top of a hill so steep that motorists followed me at a respectful distance like a funeral procession, then tooted and applauded when I reached the top.

Pant, pant.

I flash back to the impossible road up Volcán Masaya in Nicaragua, engulfed by sulphurous wisps.

Pant, pant.

I look down and see a small centipede overtake my front wheel. I decide to bail out. I turn the bike around and hit reverse. Santa Clara will elude me for the third and final time.

Back at ground zero I spot a pair of Dutch backpackers hanging out for a lift to the top. Both are young, blond, and carrying an air of worldly arrogance many pack especially for trips to Third World countries, then throw off when they go back home. Their problem, as is mine, is the lack of passing traffic on this day and the curious unwillingness of those passing to stop. I notice that this seemingly un-Cuban attitude is more pronounced near heavily touristed regions. The Dutch double have been waiting for more than two hours, and when I suggest that they try holding out a dollar for attention, they look at me as if I've suggested that they surrender their virginity to the next truckload of banana pickers.

"Veef nefer had to pay, and ve are not gunna start," sniffs the long-haired, bespectacled one.

They inform me that they are converting everything to pesos to make sure they get the cheapest deal. "Typical stingy Dutch," I find myself thinking in a flash of pure and unblessed bigotry, and hope I never run into them again.

Gradually I let go of my aborted attempt to get to Topes de Collantes, giving in to what that might say about my aging body, tenuous tenacity, and dissolving resolve, and set off on the long flat road to Cienfuegos.

• • • •

I haven't been pedaling long when a distinct hum catches my ear. Then it's gone. Then it's back. I strain my ears to catch it, but the breeze eats it. I hear it again, louder. A vision of a giant cloud of Cuban stalker bees leaps to mind.

I look behind me and see nothing, just fields and ocean and sky. Then something enters the corner of my eye, a fuzzy glinting blob moving along the ribbon of highway in my wake. It disappears behind a rise in the road, then reappears on the crest. It is the unmistakable purr of a peloton of cyclists.

Das Machine, as I coin this group of five German cyclists, catches up with my small wheels, hovering briefly like a space probe, its five pilots nodding imperceptibly. Then it rockets past like a spray of Lycra bullets shot from a red-and-yellow-spotted gun. Immediately ahead they slow again, nod to each other, and turn around and pedal back toward me. In a moment I am enveloped by the mother ship, safely docked among precision-engineered fat aluminum tubes, tinted eyeglasses, German-made waterproof panniers, and the whirr of five pairs of wheels as we accelerate to somewhere near 50 kilometers per hour.

Whew. It is hopeless. After five minutes in hyperspace, I realize that I cannot keep up and fall away like a loose cog, motioning for them to continue without me. I see them close ranks and wave *auf Wiedersehen,* and my guard of honor hums down the highway.

I am suddenly pedaling alone as before.

A truck groaning with a giant spinachy load screeches to a halt beside me, and two men jump out to ask if I want a ride. Before I can formally accept, they bodily throw me and my bike on top of the huge green cargo. My bags are hustled into the cabin.

A free ride does not come without a price, and perched atop this verdant mattress is a lecherous *hombre* who crawls across to my neck of the cabbage patch to fire a volley of questions about my marital status and sexual orientation. He then grabs my chin to extract an answer while I try to stop my bike from bouncing off the green bed. During all of this I curse myself for allowing my bags, which are riding in the front seat with my rescuers, to leave my clutches. Instead of enjoying the scenery or Spinachman's advances, I watch a mental movie of the men gleefully molesting my belongings.

I need not worry. They are basically cheerful, honest farm workers, and they drop me and my unfondled belongings about 10 kilometers from Cienfuegos. I give them 10 pesos for the trip, thankful to be out of Spinachman's grasp, and they are gone.

• • • •

I resume my meditative pedaling. It isn't too long before my ears pick up that precision purr again. Rapidly filling my rearview mirror, Das Machine looms once again. She envelops me once more, bleeps *auf Wiedersehen,* and in the next nanosecond is a receding blip into the future.

I fantasize for a split second about the five German pilots scratching their heads over a Coke in bewilderment, checking their synchronized onboard GPS gizmos to determine how I'd gotten in front of them. I know that they were scratching their heads about no such thing.

I finally arrive in Cienfuegos, where Das Machine probably landed eons earlier. A large, tree-lined square beckons, as does a group of young touts who waste no time in telling me that a room will cost $20 to $30. I stick to my guns.

"Ten dollars," I say.

I sit around, unhurried, as there is plenty of sunlight yet. The young touts lose their eagerness, one by one. A dark-skinned *muchacho* who calls himself Abraham offers me a room in his house, where I can stay for whatever I want to contribute. He does warn, however, that his little pad is located in a seedier part of town and that I will need to come around when it is dark, since there is a good chance of a policeman spotting him dabbling in the unlicensed hospitality business and slapping him with a $500 fine.

I sit some more. Eventually, Abraham offers to show me some decent *casas* nearby and help negotiate a lower rate with them. I relent.

An ornate door is opened by a couple of portly German guests, regulars at this establishment, they tell me. They inform me loudly that the rent here is $30 a night and there is no discount, *gracias y adiós*. A brief peek through the tiny gaps between them and the doorway reminds me of the rich house in Sancti Spíritus.

We find a place nearby that is $10 a night but looks downright depressing. Now well into overtime, Abraham tells me that he will take me to his aunt's licensed house. I am not sure why it took him so long to offer this option; I suspect because it's harder to extract money from one's own family.

The house is a colonial beauty in very good condition. The owners are a burly black couple and an old black woman who must be close to a century old and is lovingly referred to as *abuelita* (little grandmother). They agree on $10 a night and show me a schedule of prices: fresh juice 25 cents, cup of tea 15 cents, piece of toast 10 cents.

I have a bad feeling about this town, but I cannot quantify

it. The architecture is fine. The people are fine. The setting is fine. That is the problem. Everything is just fine, just like most other towns I have visited in the world. It takes something else to make a place special. Often, it's simply the absence of something, like tension. I decide to make the most of the day and take the bike, unloaded, for a spin down to Punta Gorda, the upscale end of the city on a peninsula.

Punta Gorda features some fine examples of 1960s seaside architecture. I see curved balconies, retro colors, and my personal favorite, a nautical-style house with panes of pale blue glass that looks ready to sail away.

I pedal down to the *malecón* and sit on the seawall to write in my diary. It is peaceful. The Bay of Cienfuegos washes up against the wall, the sun is a comfortable temperature, and slender palm trees swing and sway in the breeze. There is no one in sight. I have been sitting for about half an hour, engrossed in my journal-writing, when a black *muchacho* with a shaven head slides by and asks if I have the time. I look up, and he repeats the question.

I point to the pale strip of skin where my Casio world time watch once sat and say no. He goes and sits on the curb a little way from me, leaning his back against the curved trunk of the spindly palm, and he appears to be relaxing, doing nothing in particular. I should have twigged at this, but Cuba is so full of young *muchachos* lolling about, idly waiting for the next opportunity to make a dollar, that I think nothing of it.

After a time I hear him say something. I look up, and he has his trousers unzipped and is masturbating. I have a sudden urge to get out of there as fast as I can. Not a single humorous willy joke enters my mind.

I sigh, put my book in my bag, and go to get on my bike. In

that moment the *hombre* jumps up and runs toward me. Still masturbating with his left hand, and God knows how I register that he is left-handed, he grabs my other hand and forces it toward his crotch. I panic, experience what it is like to be held and forced by someone stronger, and scream obscenities in pure, unadulterated English until I am hoarse.

At the sound of my screaming, he clenches his fist and punches me fair square between the eyes. I feel the smack and see stars. Then he suddenly releases me and runs off, scaling the wall at the end of the street and disappearing over the other side, with me running after him in a mixture of blind fear and fury, screaming blue murder in his wake. It takes me a few seconds to register that he is gone.

At this point a couple appears, sashaying arm in arm, and asks what the problem is. Shaking, I explain what happened. They look faintly amused. The joke is the same the world over, no matter what lingo. I ask where the police station is. I want to call someone, anyone, and track down my attacker if it is the last thing on my mind before I *die*.

• • • •

I find the police station. I find a couple of policemen. I recount my tale, shaking. They laugh. Maybe I would have, too, if someone else had been telling the story.

"This may be funny to you, but it is not funny to me," I say in a level tone.

They straighten up.

"*Claro, claro.*" Of course, of course.

I get in the police car, and we drive around looking for the boy. A blue and green and white checked shirt. They rub their forearms with a finger inquiringly. Yes, he is black.

We drive around and around, but he is gone. They say that it is difficult to find someone of that description. That some people are "sick." They drop me back at the station, where my bike is parked.

I ride back to my *casa*, looking behind me all the way in case the guy is behind me. Back at the house I relate the tale to my hosts, with some care, since they are black, all three of them. I can smell my attacker on my hands, on the brim of my hat. They listen in silence. For some reason I can see only one thought whirling through their minds: *This is not good for business.*

I ask for a drink. They bring me a small glass of juice. I absentmindedly take out my wallet and put 25 cents on the table, a subconscious attempt to normalize my state of mind. My host takes the money.

Despite taking a shower, I still cannot seem to wash the stench of my assailant off my skin. I lie down and lose all desire to see more of this town.

· · · ·

In the evening Abraham comes around to say hello. After hearing my story he offers to take me out on the town to cheer me up.

"We will take one of the horse-drawn coaches," he says.

I am recovered sufficiently from my shock, and I accept.

We walk out to where the regular horse-drawn carriage passes, and he insists on paying. We clip-clop down Paseo del Prado, the long, wide avenue that runs down the center of town and into the peninsula. People are out on the streets walking, eating, moving about. Several lit buildings and movie theaters give the town a festive feel.

We get off at an outdoor disco where scores of teenagers and students have gathered to dance to rock and salsa. A mirror ball spangles the crowd. I notice the glittery, tight tops worn by the girls, bare shoulders, bare navels, bulging midriffs. The boys wear T-shirts and jeans. There is the odd guy in a suit and tie and a smattering of scruffy, older men. All of these people who have nothing more pressing to do have come to be together tonight.

I scan the crowd and freeze. I see the shirt of my attacker. I see his shaved head. But I cannot be absolutely sure that it is him.

I point the shirt out to Abraham and he shrugs. I want to go back to the safety of my rented four walls with the lock on the door. We get in the carriage again, and Abraham insists on paying again.

"Don't worry, I have money," he keeps saying. I ask how much he has.

"I have $45 in the bank," he says. "So I have money. When I don't have money, I worry. When I have money, I don't worry."

He grins.

I think of the $2,000 or so in greenback dollars in my panniers. And I worry.

20

RETURN TO HAVANA

I can't get out of Cienfuegos fast enough. In fact, I have every intention of hitching a ride on the first and fastest *camión* heading north and, if I must, paying the strictly unlawful but tacitly expected dollar gratuity five-fold, without quibbling.

Over a breakfast of rice and beans, toast, and a glass of hand-squeezed orange juice, my hosts flip through the guest book to show me the parade of ethnicity that has passed through their front door. Germany, Austria, Canada, England, Canada, Canada, France, Canada. And so on. Scrawled signatures of the curious in search of soft adventure, romance, legendary sex, or simply a firsthand opinion about the land everyone has a secondhand opinion about.

My earliest notions of Cuba were that of a dangerous, difficult place, a desolate Cold War zone, barricaded, razor-wired, piled with rubble, where you must watch your back and move about as unobtrusively as an obtrusive foreigner can. Men in Cuba smoke big, pornographic cigars. Women wear feathers and dance topless on stage. A bearded man in a Russki cap stares down from posters, teeth clenching an H. Upmann *extradivino* cigar.

When I tuned into something other than my own mental propaganda and sought advice from people who had seen Cuba from the narrow seat of a bicycle, I discovered that there were just two reasons to follow in their tire tracks: great roads, and a great people. I soon discovered that a bicycle may be the only way to get truly close to these people.

As I glance through those long-gone names in my hosts' book, I wonder if any of those guests have flashbacks to this faraway place while doing the dishes or standing in line for a cappuccino or dashing across the street back home. My hosts are proud of their guest book; it is like a window into a world that they probably will never experience firsthand, just through the stories of their guests told in halting Spanish.

Abraham comes around to say good-bye and jots down his address. When I first met him a few days ago, he was a typical Cuban tout, hustling to get me a room. Now he is a friend. He has invested considerable effort in me during my visit, finding me a place to stay, showing me the town, paying for my coach fares. For a moment I feel both guilt and gratitude, and I reach into my back pocket to take out a couple of dollars. Abraham holds up his hand in protest.

"No . . . *amistad es mejor.*" Friendship is better.

After breakfast an old man appears at the door with a rickety bicycle. My hosts have enlisted an uncle to chaperone me to the place where I can get a lift out of Cienfuegos.

"When you come back to Cienfuegos, come back here," the family chimes as I pedal away.

I do not look back as we pass the park where I had met Abraham. My eyes are still scanning for my attacker. He is nowhere to be seen. He is already a receding memory, running toward a distant wall, disappearing over the top and out of sight.

• • • •

Saturday is a bad day to hitchhike in Cuba, and Cienfuegos proves particularly tricky. I first need to get a ride 60 kilometers to Aguada de Pasajeros, the same place on the *autopista* where I passed that cold and fitful night in the plastic chair, hugging the coffee urn. Then it's another 200 kilometers to Havana.

The old uncle dutifully deposits me with a throng of stony-faced locals waiting at the lift spot, where two *amarillos* are waving down passing trucks bearing the blue number plate of the state. I offer the old man a tip, but he declines, saying that he has been "taken care of." He disappears without a smile.

The lifts are few and far between. Some trucks simply don't stop, despite much hand-waving and whistling, and on these occasions the *amarillos* leap away from the truck as it thunders by and shake their heads in disbelief. I notice that the waiting crowd remains passive; no one chides the men for not doing their job properly.

By 11:00 A.M. the best I can get is a lift on a small tray truck to a village only 7 kilometers from the highway. On the truck I sit beside a bony young woman with copper-colored skin and a resolute lower lip. She asks me where I am from and volunteers that her *esposo* comes from France. She pulls her wallet from her bag and shows me a picture of a young blond man of about thirty. He will visit her in two weeks, and yes, next year they will be married and she will go and live in France. But for now he simply visits once or twice a year and brings gifts.

I ask if they are actually married, as the word *esposo* indicates, and she nods, looking straight ahead, not smiling.

Her fingers bear no ring, just ten perfectly honed nails painted the color of *sangria*. Whether or not they are married seems immaterial. In the long waits between visits, she might as well be married, even if only in her mind, her feet shackled to Cuban soil but her heart on some Lufthansa jet. If the front gate does not squeak open at the appointed time in two weeks, there are many more where he came from.

We arrive at the village, and the woman in a Paris state of mind helps me unload my bike and bags from the truck. We wish each other luck. Leaving her and the rest of the passengers stranded and waiting for another ride, I pedal off toward the *autopista*. My heart sings for having a folding bicycle.

• • • •

Like in the film *Groundhog Day,* I find myself yet again at that crossroads. The sun is now dialing itself up to fry tortillas on the hoods of the occasional passing 1959 Chevy. One small sign grants me a slab of shade the size of a postage stamp. The highway is annoyingly silent. Cyclists hate traffic, yet this is one moment when I would pay for a traffic-choked peak hour. I hold out a dollar bill and notice that the occasional car that does appear seems to hit the gas pedal directly in front of me, as if mocking my predicament, although this is probably my heat-struck imagination.

It takes me a while to notice an old *campesino* with a sack of onions trying to get a ride. I walk over to join him, the power of two being better than one. He's been holding out a green 5-peso note for an hour, trying to get a lift a mere 20 kilometers up the road. With a shrug he sighs that 5 pesos isn't a "sufficiently attractive" traffic-stopper today.

To see the old man standing for so long, holding out money in the hope of getting a ride from his brethren, seems incongruous. This is a land where people go out of their way to help each other get milk or bread or a box of matches, yet when it comes to transport, generosity seems to cut out like a faulty ignition. This thought is confirmed when a sleek van with an empty hold slows in front of us. The driver winds down the window and peers across to see what I am offering. He recoils in disgust.

"No, not for a dollar," he sneers. "Ten dollars, *sí.*"

I offer $5.00.

"Ten," he says. I shake my sunstruck head.

The tinted window slides skywards, and the van roars off. The old *campesino* just shrugs. It seems that the spirit of hitching, the haves helping the have-nots, is fading fast everywhere on earth, and Cuba is no different. Outside the established system where state vehicles are expected to give rides for free, almost nobody wants to stop, and nobody wants to do it for love of country, company, or a less-than-decent kickback. Cash, not karma, is what mends holes in jeans and puts an extra bread roll on the table.

• • • •

After another hour of waiting for a lift, our combined $1.20 carrot starts to wither along with my patience. Suddenly, a large, state-owned truck with a long, flat tray and a handful of passengers atop rumbles past, slows abruptly, and stops just a few meters up the road. The *campesino* and I run to catch it. The driver, a young, dirty-faced boy, gets out of the cabin, comes round to the back, and holds out his hand.

"*Dinero,*" he says. I give him the dollar without questioning it. He takes it without a smile and swings himself back into the cabin. I am witnessing the oldest charity in the traveling world, the hitching system, evolve into a modern fare system.

But I am happy. I am in motion again. I am riding the same kind of truck on which my bike and I were robbed, snap frozen, and immobilized a month or so earlier, but now the wind is warm and the sky is visible and the bumps tolerable.

After a while the truck stops, and the lithe, spindly frame of a road bike is hoisted into the tray, followed by the equally lithe, spindly frame of its owner. Her name is Yoanka, and she is an athlete. She tells me that she is on the cycling team to train for the 2000 Olympics in Sydney, which will take place in just a few months.

My mind flashes back to the young drunk in Santiago who told me that he was on the Cuban boxing team headed for the same 2000 Olympics, and I remember how my host, Lolita, shook her head and rolled her eyes and complained of how Cubans are full of *mentiras* (lies).

But Yoanka has the aura of a champion. Her legs are taut and shiny like those of a well-bred racehorse, her hair is pulled back to reveal smooth, evenly tanned skin, and behind her wrap sunglasses, which she says are "Oakley copies" issued by her cycling school, I see her wide, green eyes.

Yoanka is heading back to her Sports Institute and velodrome in Cojímar, just outside Havana, where she boards and trains with several other athletes in preparation for the big international event. When she is not training, she lives on Isla de la Juventud, the island I would have visited had it not been for that loony sailor and the nightmare hitch on his 20-foot boat.

Yoanka is just twenty-four years old, married to a Cuban, and she reeks of quiet, contented confidence. Although she has traveled overseas for her sport, she says that she is happy in

Cuba and has no desire to leave her country. Well, maybe just "to visit." I can picture her sloping along on a runway in a Halston dress, or stepping out of a limousine at the Sydney Opera House, thin straps and diamonds against tanned skin.

There is an uncanny power in a young woman who can have the world, but who chooses to play on the rusty swing in her own backyard.

At her suggestion we jump off the truck about 24 kilometers from the turnoff to her school and start riding together, unfortunately at my pace. With my thirty pounds of baggage, racks, mirrors, lights, fenders, and water bottles I feel like a dump truck and ride about as fast. After 2 kilometers Yoanka comments that she's not used to riding so slow and feels like she's falling over sideways. I pick up the pace with some difficulty, and she moves behind me and starts pushing me with one strong hand on my back until we are literally flying down the highway abreast of the thundering trucks, me hanging on to my handlebars for dear life and panting like a dog.

We arrive at the institute, a big, white concrete complex with the unmistakable curved roofline of a velodrome in the background. The building houses several floors of segregated dormitories where healthy, young athletes, cultivated in the provinces of Cuba before being plucked, packed, and sent here, live and breathe finish lines and best times and the fleeting chance to plant an air-cushioned sole on foreign soil. On the ground floor is a large cafeteria where high-carb meals are dispensed on extruded trays, military mess hall style. The air is a cocktail of sporty aromas: the pungent smell of fingerless cycling gloves and rubber mats, Lycra and sweat, leather and vinyl, and rice and beans.

I am introduced to Yoanka's peers and the staff. The Chosen

Ones in the female dorm are unlike the Cuban *chicas* I have encountered thus far. These women are carbon copies of the fabulous Yoanka, cheerfully girlish yet with the focused intensity of the athletic mind, their eyes fixated on the winner's podiums tattooed inside their eyelids. They show little interest in my loaded bicycle, which sits looking fat and very slow off the mark. I can see them thinking, "What for?"

But only for one-sixteenth of a second.

. . . .

Painted on the wall outside the main entrance of the Sports Institute is a logo: *A SYDNEY POR LA GLORIA DE LA PATRIA*. To Sydney for the Glory of the Country. It's odd to see the name of my hometown painted on the wall, and spelled correctly. It feels like the world has suddenly shrunk to a size XXS.

Yoanka asks if I want to stay overnight in the dorm with the girls. I gracefully decline. There is really nothing I have in common with these intense, focused women. Their lives are about going as fast as possible, stopping to smell only the roses presented to them on the winner's dais. My life is about the exact opposite. "Be not afraid of moving too fast, but only of standing still," a friend once said, quoting an ancient Chinese monk with air-cushioned slippers. Ten miles per hour toward the nearest exit is plenty fast enough for me.

One of the staff, Roberto, offers to accompany me back to Havana on his bicycle. As I wish Yoanka luck and tell her I will come and visit her on her island one day, her husband drives up in a car to take her out for the evening. An equally handsome, muscular Cuban, his boxlike jaw is unsmiling. She slips into the passenger seat and swings her long legs inside as he carefully closes the door behind her. She smiles and waves through the tinted glass, just like in the movies.

Roberto and I pedal into the night. He rides an old mountain bike that he has managed to keep in reasonable order since he operates his own *ponchero* business in a dusty nook between a vegetable shop and a bootmaker. We ride to where the bicycle bus will take us over the no-cyclists-allowed bridge.

This seems an extremely civilized setup. We wait in a sheltered place until a very well-maintained bus with no seats and ample handrails drives up. We are loaded into its spacious cabin one by one. It seems to be another of the anomalies of Cuba: People go underground to get a daily half liter of milk, which they must water down for their babies, yet a modern bus with a pneumatic door and strip lighting whisks decrepit old bicycles across a bridge on a regular schedule.

• • • •

By night, Havana seems menacing.

The absence of street lighting in all but the main boulevards forces me to ride by feel of cobble against rubber, and now and then I am blinded completely by the headlights of an oncoming car swinging across my path. The black skyline is punctuated only by the odd glowering tourist hotel, its roofline illuminated with kitsch blue or pink neon tube lighting.

In my handlebar bag is the address of Kenia, sister-in-law of Zaida, whom I stayed with in Manzanillo. Roberto helps me locate the right house, marked by a narrow, weathered double door, and then bids me goodnight. I tell him I'll come and visit him at his bicycle repair shop. He disappears while I am still speaking.

I buzz the button and wait.

I buzz again. I hear noises. It is an old apartment building with polished cement floors and chipped walls. The door opens to reveal Kenia, a tall, part-Chinese woman. She listens patiently while I introduce myself and retell my story, now tinged with just a hint of weariness. She opens the door wider to let me in.

Maybe I've been doing this for too long, for I now start to feel less like I did a few weeks ago, less like an exotic visitor from another planet bringing a ray of freedom and sunshine to the wretched and limited lives of the average Cuban. Now I feel like a haggard and self-interested freeloader trying to get by on charity.

I reason that this could simply be the Big City Effect, which seems to exist whether you are talking about Havana, Sydney, New York, or Kabul. Someone once explained it in terms of compression. When space, money, and time are compressed, as in a big city, people feel compressed, and the first thing to get squeezed is the ability to give your fellow human the time of day. Cuba is unique, but as people, Cubans are not immune to the Big City Syndrome.

• • • •

Kenia lives with her husband, José, an open-heart surgeon, and their teenage niece, Kattya. Kattya works in a cigar factory, and when she hears that I bought twenty-five cigars on the street for $2.50, she wrinkles her nose and presents me with a single unlabeled Montecristo to give to someone very special.

José earns $25 a month as a surgeon; Kenia does not work. They have only recently moved to Havana from Manzanillo to seek a better life. She tells me that people who live in Havana get more rations from the government than those in the rest of the country, presumably because of the higher cost of living.

For dinner they invite me to share some tomato slices, a fried egg, and some leftover salad, served on white foam meat trays saved from the supermarket, which are carefully washed and reused as dinner plates. Unfine china.

They show me where I will sleep, with their niece in a bedroom behind a curtain. It has a standard Cuban light switch: two long thin wires hanging from the ceiling that ignite a spluttering fluorescent tube when touched together.

• • • •

"Time to rise and shine . . ."

I wake in the morning to the burble of an electronic voice. It repeats itself every fifteen minutes or so until I know that it cannot be the television. I stumble to feel for the wires to turn on the light. Kattya is still asleep. I follow the electro-voice into the darkened room next door. The last thing I expect to see is the large computer sitting on a table in Kenia's bedroom, with multicolored tropical fish sliding across the screen. Now and then a frog with a pocket watch pops up and tells whoever is listening that it's "time to rise and shine."

José and Kenia are already up and puttering about. He explains that he has performed many operations on foreigners living in Cuba, and to express their gratitude, a group of them banded together and bought him a personal computer. He can't access the Internet, nor does it have much software, but it does tell the time in a most optimistic manner. One day they will have the Internet.

On the kitchen table are a couple of leftover slices of tomato and two pieces of toast for my breakfast. I pack and leave $10 on the table for the family. Kenia stares at the money.

"Why?" she asks.

"To help you," I answer.

"You're a good person, Lynette," she says without a smile. I look at this family and their foam-meat-tray dinner plates sitting in the dish rack and feel distinctly unworthy of such an accolade.

From Kenia's house it is a short ride back to Maruca's *casa particular*, to my bicycle suitcase and return ticket to Costa Rica. I cram my bike into the dusty elevator and push the button for her floor.

The door opens, and Maruca puts her hands to her mouth and squeals. She drags me inside. "Why did you not call? I was worried!" she exclaims.

Then she immediately slips back into the magazine she was reading.

• • • •

I've come full circle. It is like I never left Maruca's apartment. I find my bicycle suitcase in the cupboard where I left it three months ago. I set about repacking my gear, although there is really nothing much to do, because when you are on the road for so long you can't help but put things in the right place and discard rubbish and silly souvenirs as you go.

That evening, Maruca asks if I want to go to her Bautista church service.

"There will be lots of singing!" she exclaims.

"We can go get ice cream from Coppelia," I declare. "My treat."

We take several buses and trams to get to the church, about

half an hour away. When we arrive the service is well under way. Around fifty people, young and old, sit quietly in plastic chairs, listening to the intense young man in the pulpit.

I guess that he is twenty-five or so. A Puerto Rican, says Maruca. Apparently Puerto Ricans are increasingly popular recruits in the evangelistic business: articulate, charismatic, and possessed of swarthy yet angelic good looks—the modern-day multicultural representatives of your favorite savior.

The lad implores the gathering to examine the notions of faith and integrity, and judging from the rapture of the audience, he does the Father, Son, Holy Ghost, and all their in-laws proud. His voice quivers with emotion as he presents a concept, rises to a shout for emphasis, then drops to a whisper as he repeats himself, clasping his hands to his heart and squeezing his eyes tightly lest a tear escape. He has a tan. After more than an hour of his impassioned pleas, I feel unenlightened and hampered by my rudimentary Spanish, and I start to get a numb butt from the hard plastic chair. I lean toward Maruca.

"Feel like Coppelia?" I whisper.

Maruca sits transfixed, and she motions for me to keep quiet.

After another half an hour of this relentless sermon, Maruca turns to me.

"I can't take anymore," she sighs. "Let's go to Coppelia."

• • • •

We leave the service midcrescendo and head down the street, dotted with people who have just reemerged after the evening's episode of *la novela*.

In Coppelia we order the flavor of the day, vanilla. A friend of Maruca's pops by to say hello. In her hand is a plastic lunch box in which six scoops of ice cream are trying their best to stay hard until she makes it back home to her children.

"I don't know what happened to the singing tonight," laments Maruca, "They normally preach a little, and then the rest of it is singing. Wonderful singing . . ."

I tell Maruca that I find it hard to give the young evangelist much credence. I explain that he is way too young. In my twenties I thought I knew it all, but I have since discovered that I knew nothing. I know little more now. I explain my path to enlightenment: to live life as it occurs, and to take the hard knocks. Each knock gives you a tool to swing at the next hard knock. So how can I take advice from a kid for whom the hardest knock is probably being dead-legged on the soccer field, and who probably chews gum to look cool rather than to freshen his breath? I reason that this twenty-something Puerto Rican lay preacher, like all kids, must be brimming with the insecurities that nature piles on thick in our twenties so that we'll all procreate like a good species ought.

I warm to my self-indulgent post-Darwinian theorizing. No, nature does not give a damn about "finding ourselves" and traveling aimlessly and having careers and dreams. Nature just wants us to have sex and further the species.

"Ahhhh," says Maruca patiently. "True, he knows less of life than you. But the difference is, he has known God."

I meditate on this as I go to order another serve of ice cream.

There is no more.

21

ONE LAST SCOOP

Somewhere in Pinar del Río sits a box of ordinary Cuban cigars with my name on it.

The cost of the box and its pungent contents is exactly $2.50, plus I'll have to add at least a couple of long days bike-hitching to collect it. It makes sense to forget about the cigars since I am not going to smoke them and neither will most of the people to whom I might offer them as souvenirs of my Cuba trip. And the thought of once again sweltering in a queue on an open highway fills me with a profound lethargy. These thoughts are running through my head as I languish in a chair, letting *la novela* on the television lull me into a Zen-like state of wondering if the *picaflor* really did cheat on his fiancée or . . .

I know that people in Pinar del Río are waiting on my return. I know that I have entrusted Carlos, the voice of lunchtime radio soap opera, with my $2.50 to effect my cigar order with his secret supplier, and that my friends Ana and Nieves are keeping them safe for me. I know that they will not let me down. I snap out of *la novela* and out of my chair.

Instead of taking the leisurely coastal route out of Havana, as I did the first time around, I opt to try for a fast ride down the *autopista*. Once again I wedge my fully loaded bike into the small elevator. On the third floor a fat woman with a small dog tries to get in. There is a moment of consternation.

"Why don't you take the stairs?" she says reproachfully.

Today the streets of Havana are bustling, but in a low-key way. I set out a little nervously because years of bicycle touring have never improved my sense of direction. At every street corner I confirm the directions with whomever happens to be propping up the nearest lamppost. I head south past the Plaza de la Revolución, where a giant line drawing of Che Guevara rendered in wrought iron leaps iconically from the face of a building. I exit onto Avenida Rancho Boyero, then take Calle 100 all the way to the *autopista*. Before too long I am doing battle with giant, belching, rattling trucks thundering along Calle 100, which must be the busiest road in Cuba. Thankfully there is a generous shoulder.

I finally reach the *autopista,* a desolate, gray ribbon of concrete disappearing westward. Cubans are already dotted randomly along its shoulders with their various sacks and baskets. Their heads are wrapped in scarves, and they tote half-filled backpacks. I fold the bike and stand there with my thumb out.

A tsunami of déjà vu engulfs me. Empirical evidence suggests that three months is about my time limit for a single trip before new things suddenly get old. As I wait with one toe stabbing the concrete, I have ample time to theorize about why the *autopista* is not a good place to snag a lift after all: People take the soulless fast lane to save time. They are not interested in stopping and have even less interest in conversation with a stranger. Even for $1.00. Even for $5.00.

• • • •

I stand near a brother and sister who say that they hitch this same 147-kilometer route to and from Pinar del Río for work every second day. Today they've been waiting for a ride since 7:00 A.M. It is now midday.

Around 1:00 P.M. a truck bound for San Cristobal, halfway to Pinar del Río, stops in front of us and we make a run for it. We are each plied for 10 pesos. As I settle into the truck bed, I play a little game with myself. Can I make this one last trip and have nothing stolen? I sit in the tray and watch everything like a hawk, including the coal-colored guy opposite whose eyes are fixed on my bike, as if he is studying what is most easily finger-unscrewable.

The trip is blessedly uneventful, another bumpy, windy ride with a large, dirty rubber tire wedged into my lower back. When I jump off I take stock of everything and breathe a sigh of relief. Nothing missing, mission complete.

I reach for my trusty sun visor, one of those kitsch neoprene jobs with the stretchy telephone-cord strap that are sold in drugstores. It is a perfect hair restrainer for a long-haired cyclist. It is gone from my handlebars. I also notice that the nice rubber-covered quick release lever on the front of my bike has somehow been switched for a cheaper, less ergonomic one.

For the life of me I cannot work out when or how this could have happened. The only time I left my bike on its own was in Havana, but it was in my direct line of sight through a bar window and under the requested surveillance of two policemen. The day before I had used that lever to fold my bike, and I clearly recall the feel of rubber against palm. This one is cold and metallic to the touch.

"*Lo hacen,*" shrugs a wiry local who stops to ask me why I am staring so intently at the lever. They do it.

He looks at me and asks, "Are you married?"

I tell him yes.

"Where is your husband, then?"

I sigh. I am entering the third and final phase of this trip, and the Cuban-style mating game is getting old, very old.

I make it to Pinar del Río by midafternoon with a mixture of rides and fast pedaling. Ana and her mother are not at home when I finally find their house, but the door is unlatched.

I decide that it is time to become invisible to the Don Juans once and for all.

I dig out a crumpled shirt and cotton trousers with dirty tooth marks down the right leg caused by my bicycle chain. I find an orange mesh bag used by Cuban women to tote their bread rolls and ration book. Instead it holds my camera and guidebook doubly concealed in a white plastic bag. My stained and floppy canvas hat, cheap dark glasses, and frayed beach sandals complete the "please ignore me" outfit.

Ana suddenly appears from her bedroom, immaculately turned out in her employer-issued uniform for another day at the Dollar Fashion Boutique. She runs to embrace me, then jumps back to gape in amusement at my disguise.

I hold my breath and shuffle along the sidewalk, stealing covert glances at the males lounging against fences and lampposts.

I can feel their eyes on me as I pass. Each time I successfully pass a male and not a single courting hiss emerges from his lips, I feel a rush of excitement. I make it to the corner unhissed. Have I finally become a true Cubana?

I wear this costume right up until the day I fly out of Cuba.

Construction workers fail to notice me. Passing cars do not toot. Men do not approach me to strike up a conversation about marriage and/or emigration. I purchase a tub of ice cream from a dollar store and mosey along the street in a solitary daydream, eating spoonfuls while contemplating my beautiful, anonymous Cuban life.

A woman approaches me and points excitedly at my ice-cream tub.

"Where did you get that?"

"From the dollar store," I say.

She does a double take, then smiles.

"Oh, you're not Cuban?" she asks.

I tingle again, and in gratitude I give her my ice cream.

As I turn to head back to the house and my waiting lift to the airport, I pass a tall, black man slouched against a tree, and his eyes follow me.

"*China, bella, linda,*" he whispers. Lovely, beautiful Chinese girl.

Dang.

22

HOME?

I sit in the Lacsa plane with my head against the window. Cuba slowly rolls by below my right cheek. I gaze down at María La Gorda, the westernmost tip of the island where I had pitched my tent before accepting that hellish boat ride. María the Voluptuous Woman moves by and fades into the distance. Cuba, the land beneath the wing, vanishes in a sea of turquoise froth. I squint. I can almost see, far, far below, the rows of flat pebbles that I used to make a little pathway to my tent on Cayos de San Felipe.

The officials at the Havana airport had smiled as they stamped a little piece of paper that told anyone who'd cared to fish it out of the recycling bin that I had been a visitor to Cuba. They asked me to return soon.

As I watch Cuba recede over the horizon, I reflect upon how my preconceived opinions of this country compare with my firsthand observations. I imagined barb-wire barricades. No barricades, no barbed wire, no overt military presence. I imagined starvation. No desperate hunger, no overt poverty, no disease. No frightened faces or loud antigovernment protests, firebombs, or riots. Nothing bloody, homeless, starving, or loud.

Just a single, invisible leash that loops gently around the neck of every Cuban, from one to the next, long enough to join them as a nation, loose enough to allow each man, woman, and child to move through a life of love and work and the occasional *langosta escondida,* but taut enough to press on the nerve that says *I want change.*

I arrive back in Costa Rica just a couple of hours later. My bags swing off the carousel, and there is nobody there to greet me. The Tico taxi drivers rush me for my foreigner fare, not realizing that I am a resident. I take a taxi through the city to the apartment that I am renting. The streets are full of people and buses and cars, honking, begging, shouting, swarming about in a haze of blue exhaust fumes. A man is unconscious in a gutter, oblivious to a bus bearing down on his unchosen rest spot.

I dig around in several places for the keys I have not used in three months and try to remember how to open the triple-locked, 8-foot-high jail bars that encase the entire driveway and front entrance, complete with razor wire overhead. As usual, the driveway is jammed with the three or four imposing four-wheel-drive vehicles owned by the family I rent from. One of the vehicles is unfamiliar; it looks brand new. Costa Rica, the Switzerland of Latin America. The next-door neighbor is out watering his garden, and he keeps his eyes on the hose. The resident maid smiles briefly but disappears into the adjoining house where my landlady lives.

On the answering machine is one lone message, from my boss. Apparently my landlady has complained to him about the "bad people" she had seen me invite into my apartment before I left for Cuba. She was referring to Heidi and Joel, the American-Venezuelan couple whom I had befriended months earlier in the Caribbean.

Heidi is white. Joel is black. They wear the vibrant, traditional clothing from his homeland and earn a living by making jewelry, including the coconut-shell hair clasp they gave me as thanks for my friendship. I go downstairs to take up the grievance with my landlady. She has not noticed that I have been away, as I paid my rent for three months in advance. When I ask her about the message, she throws up her hands in false ignorance.

"I don't know who told your boss that, but there are children here and we cannot have these dangerous people here. Perhaps you should look for another apartment."

She shuts the door gently in my face.

BICYCLING IN CUBA

Semi-Technical Stuff

INFORMATION RESOURCES

There are many Web sites and books about Cuba to trawl over while you are deciding what to pack. I prefer to research just enough to get enthused, but not confused.

www.cyberbub.pwp.blueyonder.co.uk/steve/cuba.htm
¡Viva Cuba!
Stephen Psallidas's Web site is a succinct and very useful account for the gung-ho touring cyclist. He made it to the top of Topes de Collantes, so he has a better pair of calves than I do.

www.geocities.com/TheTropics/Shores/5902
Allison's Budget Travel Guide to Cuba
Allison did a three-week backpacking trip in 1996, and since little has changed in Cuba compared to other countires, her site is worth reading for the same kind of lucid, incisive commentary as Stephen's. It's slightly more upscale, which is good for when the bucket baths get to be too much.

www.womenwelcomewomen.org.uk
Women Welcome Women World Wide
Based in England, this is a mutual hospitality and friendship club for traveling women in seventy countries. Ladies, never feel hesitant about landing in a strange place again!

Selected guidebooks, listed by publisher:
Bradt: *Cuba*
Globe Pequot: *Traveler's Companion Cuba*
Lonely Planet: *Cuba*
Lonely Planet: *Cycling Cuba*
New Holland: *Cuba Travel Pack*
Thomas Cook: *Travellers Cuba*

GEAR AND SUPPLIES

What follows is a list of items I found useful for my Cuba trip and for bicycle touring in general.

My bicycle
Bike Friday New World Tourist, 21-speed, black
www.bikefriday.com

Bike Friday USA makes the world's leading performance travel bicycle. Each bike folds in seconds, packs into an airline-checkable suitcase, and is custom-fitted for the individual rider. The 20-inch wheels make the bike lighter, faster, and easier to turn, climb, and accelerate—and no, you don't have to pedal more; the gear ratios make it equivalent to riding a regular-size bike. Many celebs of the cycling world have a Bike Friday in the back of their car or closet. Former *Bicycling USA* magazine editor Ed Pavelka (one luminary of www.roadbikerider.com)

says Bike Friday "rides as good as your best bike."

It's also the perfect bike for women, being scalable due to the smaller wheels. You can order a Bike Friday by e-mail or phone, and in about four weeks it will arrive on your doorstep, no matter where you live. I ordered mine while in Australia. Best of all, you instantly make friends with this unique machine. Don't go trying to grapple with big wheels and airline fees before you at least take a look at a Bike Friday. And no, Bike Friday did not sponsor me on this trip.

My saddle
Terry Ti Men's Fly
www.terrybicycles.com

I have been through so many saddles trying to find one that fits that I could safely be called the Posterial Imelda Marcos. However, I have learned that bike fit and riding position affect butt comfort more than the throne itself. I solved the fit problem by buying a Bike Friday. I solved the comfort problem by making sure my handlebars are at least level with the seat, thus distributing weight more evenly between the three points: feet, butt, hands. This saddle seems to flex enough in the middle, plus the longer nose of the men's version lets you carry the bike on your shoulder if necessary.

My pedals
Shimano Dual Function
http://bike.shimano.com

These clunkers are heavy, but it's useful having SPD clips on one side and a flat other side for sandals and normal shoes. I even added a pair of Powergrips to the flat side, which are straps to slip your feet into while wearing sandals or running shoes.

My clothing and shoes

Assos, Lake, Chaco

www.assos.com

www.lakecycling.com

www.chacousa.com

Good cycling gear is an investment. I have been wearing my black Assos Roubaix jacket and red Swiss flag jersey for years. They're always the right weight and stay warm when wet. I like to use Pace legwarmers, which you can roll down to your ankles if it gets hot and you don't want to grapple with overtights. I wore Lake SPD mountain bike shoes for this trip. This kind of dual-function shoe is neither the best cycling shoe nor the best hiking shoe, but does an okay job of both. Dual-functionality is key—it allows you to carry less stuff.

Sandals that you can use on land and in the sea—and that still look good at dinner—are the holy grail. I haven't found them yet. They'd be black and stylish, with quick-drying straps. Chaco sandals come close, though they still look like Jesus boots.

My bags

Ortlieb Back-Roller Waterproof Panniers

www.ortlieb.com

I swear that these panniers are as tough and as waterproof as they come. I like the heavier, shiny ones; dirt wipes off them easier. On the front I have a little Tioga handlebar bag, a cheap faded thing that hangs on for dear life by two Velcro straps. I put a large Ziploc plastic bag inside to hold anything I want to stay dry. There are many fancier click-release waterproof bags, but I like to keep things simple. In fact, Ortlieb makes a fabulous waterproof map case, but in fairly dry weather, a folded map in a plastic Ziploc bag is just as easy to whip out of your pocket. Vaude is another brand that makes a similar bag (www.vaude.com).

My stove
The smallest, simplest Trangia stove
www.trangia.se

This stove is fueled by methylated spirits (the term used in Australia), or whatever alcohol you can lay your hands on, and a match. It is no bigger than an instant ramen-noodle container but perfect for a decent serving of banana-raisin-nut porridge, instant soup mix, veggies and pasta, even bread pudding (of sorts—just combine leftover bread, muesli, milk powder, eggs, whatever). Make sure you put a little water in the meths to stop your pot from going black. You can get fancier multifuel stoves these days, but the simple model did the job for me.

My tent
Macpac Microlite
www.macpac.co.nz

This little pod accommodates one and a half people and weighs around one and a half kilograms, or three pounds. The only problem is that it is not freestanding, so don't try pitching it on a tarmac. I found it to be totally waterproof in a week of downpour in Seathwaite, designated as the wettest place in England. The tent is made in New Zealand, where it rains a lot. For hot- weather countries consider an ultralight expedition hammock (www.hennessyhammock.com).

My sleeping bag

Mont three-season

www.mont.com.au

I did not take this bag to Cuba, as it was too warm. I would recommend one of the new ultralight sleeping bags that have a sleeve you slip your mat into, so that all the feathery filling is on top. For my Cuba trip I took a couple of airline blankets to which I sewed snap fasteners to clip them together. This is a good warm-weather option, and they fold flat. The blankets were subsequently purloined by a Nicaraguan maid in Costa Rica, which serves me right since I stole them in a fury from the airline that took two days instead of two hours to get me home from Miami.

My mat

Therm-a-rest Ultralite

www.thermarest.com

Although I am only 5 feet tall, I wish I'd bought the full-length mat. Nothing is more disconcerting than having your feet on the tent floor when the rest of you is cushioned by the mat. Yes, you can stick your jacket under your feet, but honestly, go full length. I also have the accessory that turns the mat into a chair; this makes it easy on your lower back if you've allowed enough time in your schedule to lounge about.

OTHER ITEMS FOR YOUR KIT

Local road atlas: The most useful one by far is the Guía de Carreteras, an incredibly detailed forty-eight-page 1:300,000 road atlas of Cuba showing all roads and contours in full color. Available from most car rental places in Cuba for $5.00.

Soap: Put a small piece in a plastic pillbox in your pocket. The easiest way to stay healthy on the road is to keep your hands clean.

Alcohol: 95-percent alcohol for cuts, bites, and scrapes and for cleaning and sterilizing hands and objects. Easier and less messy to use than fancy lotions and creams, alcohol can be used in place of soap when there is no water. Keep it in the handlebar bag.

Roll of electrical tape: For fixing holes in equipment, tent, map case, etc.

Earplugs: To block out the amorous sounds of lovers, martyred pigs . . .

Insect repellent: Carry *strong* insect repellent that kills everything except you. I do not like the idea of slathering DEET on my skin, but it is the only thing that seems to work. A little on a cloth to wipe the zip of your tent will deter micro-bugs from breaking and entering.

Toilet paper: Take out the cardboard center to make it squash flatter, or buy the tubeless variety from camping stores. Store in a small plastic bag. Sometimes I carry paper napkins instead.

Damp cloth: Store in a plastic bag in your handlebar bag for wiping hands after scoffing trail mix, etc. Keep it rinsed.

Thin balaclava: Most heat is lost through the top of your head. A balaclava doubles as a cap when rolled up.

Thermal underwear: Useful for drying your hair without getting pneumonia. Simply zip up your tent and wrap your head in whatever piece of the underwear is cleanest, and the heat of evaporation will dry your hair enough by morning.

Neoprene sun visor: Excellent for wearing with a helmet and keeping the hair off your face. It usually comes with a coiled elastic. And unlike a helmet visor, you can wear it when you are not wearing your helmet. It means you will look like an American tourist, but them's the breaks.

Little black dress: A long, simple, packable black dress with shoestring straps. You don't have to look like a traveler just because you're traveling. Multifunctional, serving as formalwear, sleepwear, beachwear, and partywear. Roll down the top, and it becomes a skirt. Optional for guys.

Overshirt: Offers protection from sun and bugs while you are riding, beachcombing, etc. Any long-sleeve white shirt will do.

Sarong: Triples as a beach towel, skirt, and shawl. Take two; keep one squeaky clean to use as a bath towel.

Silk sleep sheet: Insulates you against bedbugs on those nights you forgo the tent for a spot of dingy hostel luxury. Very compact.

Outdoor clothesline: The stretchy kind, with a carabiner at each end. But don't leave it hanging on the fence, as I have done thrice.

Machete: Optional. Useful for opening coconuts to drink the water, parting the waves on crowded trains, or reshaping the dirt track to your cabin. Be sure to stow it in checked luggage. If you have a Bike Friday, slide it into the suitcase.

Ortlieb folding bowl: A marvel of modern vinyl engineering, useful for everything from washing up to taking an APC (armpits and crutch) bath.

Ziploc bags: The small freezer kind is indispensable for storing food, for saving shells and stones that you should leave for the next eco-tourist to enjoy, and for keeping your camera and passport dry. You'd be amazed at what you stick in these bags.

Universal sink plug: A common travel guide suggestion, and for good reason.

Headlamp: Petzl makes an LED headlamp with a strong

white light and batteries that last more than one hundred hours. Buy one from your local camping store.

Candle in a tin: For some kind of light when your lamp batteries die. Don't forget matches.

Leukoplast silk tape: Never leave home without this $2.00 answer to blisters before they even think of forming.

ABOUT THE AUTHOR

When she was thirty-four Lynette Chiang fled a decent job, three-bedroom house, fast car, and nice bloke in Sydney and, armed with a poor sense of direction, set off to see the world on a folding bicycle. She has traveled solo ever since, living and working in Britain, Ireland, Nicaragua, Costa Rica, Panama, Cuba, Mexico, Peru, and the United States. Her distinguished careers have included that of computer programmer, failed waitress, Cannes award–winning copywriter, creative director of an advertising company, and manager of a mountaintop reserve—not to mention swanning around Windsor Castle dressed as an English lady.

In conjunction with Race Across America ultracyclist Lon Haldeman, Lynette shot and produced two feature-length documentaries using a simple digital camera. "16,000 Feet on a Friday: Biking the World's Highest Paved Road," was voted Audience Choice at the 2005 Boston Bike Film Festival. Lynette's latest film is "Route 66 by Bicycle: Biking the Mother Road."

Lynette was recently named one of Forbes.com's "Rugged Individualists" and has been cited in business marketing press for her innovative work in "customer evangelism." Her efforts led to Bike Friday topping the worldwide Saatchi & Saatchi Lovemarks poll and appearing in Kevin Roberts's book *The Lovemarks Effect: Winning in the Consumer Evolution.*

The National Library of Australia recently selected Lynette's Web site GalFromDownUnder.com for its national heritage archive, deeming it one of the country's "electronic publications of lasting cultural and research value."